CURIOSITIES
of
ESSEX

being glimpses of Essex history

as seen from broadside ballads

Containing over fifty ballads newly reprinted

D. OCCOMORE

IAN HENRY PUBLICATIONS

1984

© copyright, David M Occomore, 1984

ISBN 86025 885 8

Printed by the Wembley Press, Reading
for Ian Henry Publications Ltd
38 Parkstone Avenue, Hornchurch, Essex RM11 3LW

INTRODUCTION

The broadside ballad in the British Isles has been in existence for some four centuries. During this time the subject matter has covered nearly every topic imaginable, much like our newspapers of today. The broadside ballad (the contents of the sheets were usually in verse) reported current events, love stories and murders, there were political and religious sheets, wars and victories, disasters and celebrations, in fact every topic under the sun found a place on these ballad sheets.

Essex has always had a very close relationship with the broadside ballad and so I felt, having looked at the traditional songs of the county, it was time to make a follow-on study of its broadside ballads.

I sincerely hope that reading this book will provide an understanding of broadside ballad sheets, their content, and the value of this type of literature when delving into our past history.

The task of collecting material has been formidable; many of the sheets have been stored in library collections that have never been indexed and so it has been just a matter of diligently scrutinising every sheet in turn and to check its contents. When ballads have been found, there has been no convenient date that could be used for locating further details, so a large amount of detective work has been necessary to pinpoint the exact date and event that has been written about.

I have not, of course, examined every possible collection of Broadside Ballads. There are still many to be searched through and probably many more ballads will come to light when this is done.

I have kept the text more or less in historical sequence and, because of the vast amount of material available, the ballads to the 18th and 19th centuries. I have not included detailed history of the broadside ballad, as this has been thoroughly and more ably carried out by others before me, but have tried to give enough background to put the subject into perspective for my purposes here.

In writing this book it has been necessary to draw on many sources for material. To acknowledge all these individually would be a tremendous task, so I would like to thank all those who have contributed with help and suggestions.

I am also greatly indebted to a number of other writers for use of quotations from their books; these have been acknowledged at the appropriate places in the text.

As most of my researches have been made in various library collections, I would like to give special mention to the staff of the British Library for their fast retrieval of material from the archives, to the Librarian of the Vaughan Williams Memorial Library at Cecil Sharp House for so much undivided attention at various times, the Westminster Central Reference Library for their help with micro films of *The Times*, the Librarian of St Bride's Printing Library who helped me with so many enquiries over the telephone and in person, the Curator of the Thurrock Local History Museum, the Essex Records Office, Valence House Library, Colchester Library, local studies department, the Chelmsford & Essex Museum for their help with various photocopies, Waltham Abbey Historical Society for tracing information about the Royal Gunpowder Factory, Lord Bottomley for assistance in locating material at the Houses of Parliament libraries, and lastly to my wife for her patience and encouragement during the many hours spent writing up the manuscript.

D OCCOMORE. 1984

BEGINNINGS OF THE BALLAD TRADE

The printed broadside ballad began its life almost immediately after the introduction of printing and gained its first popularity in Elizabethan England when many hundreds were printed and sold.

The broadsheet or broadside was a single sheet of paper at first folio size and later a narrow strip or in quarto. Printed on coarse paper, on only one side, with either verse or prose, many with a woodcut illustration. The type used on these early broadsheets is what is now known as Old English and was very similar to the Gothic type which has continued to be used in Germany up until the present. Because of the overall appearance of the sheet, verses printed in this method became known as the black letter ballads and even long after books used Roman type, ballads were still printed in this English font. It was typographically unattractive and the author's responsibility seemed to end when his ballad was sent to the printers. He never had a desire to proofread and the printer rarely thought it necessary. As many ballads were topical, a certain amount of speed was needed in getting them printed and ready for sale, so often the letter 'W' was made up of two letter 'V's' put together. The rough woodcuts used for illustrating these sheets were often used over and over again, not always appropriate to the context of the ballad.

In the latter part of Elizabeth I's reign the broadside ballad had become one of the chief publications of the printing presses and were circulated in enormous numbers. Books were for rich upper classes and beyond the reach of most ordinary people, not only because of the price, but also through lack of leisure time to study them.

Books then shaped the life and thought of cultured people, while ballad sheets catered for the masses. Although some broadsides were in prose the main output was in verse. In 1588 William Webbe wrote in his *Discourse of English Poetry:*

"Among the innumerable sortes of English books and infinite fardles of printed pamphlets, wherewith the Country is pestered, all shops stuffed and every study furnished. The greater part I think in any one kind are such as are either mere poeticall or which tend in some respect (as either in matter or form) to poetry."

As the output of the printing trade grew, so some kind of control had to be instigated before the presses became powerful and got out of hand. So, on the 4th of May, 1557, the Stationers' Company was formed.

The Stationers' Company became the official authority over the whole country and was responsible for its members and in the future almost all decrees as to the printing and sale of books and ballads were issued to the masters or wardens of the Company, who had to see that they were carried out by members. All ballads and books were licensed and entered into the register. Up to 1588, the fee for a ballad was 4 pence, thenceafter a fee of 6 pence ($2\frac{1}{2}$p) was charged.

The broadside ballad has always been sold for 1 penny or, where a sheet with two ballads on it was split, at $\frac{1}{2}$d each.

They were hawked round city streets, village fairs and town and country markets, in fact, anywhere a crowd could be gathered.

"Ballads my masters, ballads. Will ye ha' any ballads o' the newest and truest matter in all London. I hae of them for all people and of all arguments too. Here be your story ballads, your nice maidens, your grave seniors and all sorts of men beside. Ballads! my master, rare ballads. Take a fine new ballad sir with a picture to 't'."*

*The Exchange in its Humours by B J in **A garland for the new Royal Exchange** 1669 No XIV reprint of 1845, pp. 44-5.

A typical ballad seller of this period is characterised by Shakespeare in his play *Winter's Tale* where in Act IV, Scene IV, we find Autolycus selling ballads to country folk:

Clown   What hast here? Ballads?

Mopsa   Pray now, buy some: I have a ballad in print o'life for then we are sure they are true.

Aut   Here's one to a very doleful tune, how a usurer's wife was brought to bed of twenty money bags at a burthen and how she longed to eat adders' heads and toads carbonadoed.

Mop   Is it true, think you?

Aut   Very true and but a month old.

Dorcas   Bless me for marrying a usurer!

Aut   Here's the midwife's name to't, one Mistress Taleporter, and five or six honest wives that were present. Why should I carry lies abroad?

Mop   Pray now, buy it.

Clo   Come on, buy it buy: and let's first see more ballads will buy the other things anon.

Aut   Here's another ballad of a fish that appeared upon the coast on Wednesday the fourscore of April, forty thousand fathom above water, and sang this ballad against the hard hearts of maids: it was thought she was a woman and was turned into a cold fish for she would not exchange flesh with one that loved her: the ballad is very pitiful and as true.

Dor   Is it true too think you?

Aut   Five justices' hands at it and witnesses more than my pack will hold.

Clo   Lay it by too; another.

Aut   This is a merry ballad, but a very pretty one.

Mop   Let's have some merry ones.

Aut   Why, this is a passing merry one and goes to the tune of 'Two maids wooing a man'; there's scarce a maid westward but she sings it; 'tis in request, I can tell you.

Mop   We can both sing it: if thou wilt bear a part, thou shalt hear; 'tis in three parts.

Dor   We had the tune on't a month ago.

Aut   I can bear my part; you must know it is my occupation. Have at it with you.

ANNE TURNER,
EXECUTED AT TYBURN, Nov. 15, 1615.

The ballad singer would offer to teach the tune to his customers like Autolycus, but as the title of the tune was nearly always printed at the top of the sheet and was usually one of the latest dance tunes, most of his customers would know it already.

Elizabethan Essex did not escape the attention of ballad singers. Henry Chettle in his pamphlet *Kind Harts Dream* of 1592, tells us of 'idle youths singing and selling ballads, in every corner of cities and market towns and especially at fairs and markets and such like public meetings.' Continuing: 'Now ballads are abusively chanted in every street and from London this evil has overspread Essex and the adjoining counties.' He complains that stationers who take on apprentices teach them to sing and then send them out, after about two months, with bundles of ballads to sell.

We are fortunate that we even know the names of two of the ballad singers who sang in Essex. One, a boy, named Cheeke, and nicknamed Outroaring Dick, gave up his mechanics' trade to sing ballads; his chief rival, Wat Winbas, was celebrated for singing doleful tragedies throughout Essex and neighbouring shires. Both made twenty shillings a day singing at Braintree Fair.

The methods of the ballad singer altered very little. New ballads were always in production, though the ballad printers always kept a stock of traditional folk songs printed on ballad sheets. Like the tales of Robin Hood and the deeds of Lord Bateman, they had no trouble in selling them. On the other hand, entirely new ballads had to be pushed by the sellers' patter; this was sometimes assisted by thhe ballad title that proclaimed it to be 'A new song' or some other appropriate caption and even the first verse, like 'The Ballad of the Cloak' in *Roxburge Ballads* IV, page 605, expresses the fact of its newness:

> *Come buy my new ballet I have't in my wallet*
> *But 'twill not I fear, please ev'ry pallet*
> *Then mark what ensu'th I swear by my youth*
> *That every line in my ballad is truth*
> *A ballad of wit a brave ballad of worth*
> *'Tis newly printed and newly come forth.*

Another factor that sold ballads to the Elizabethan public was if the ballad was true. In *Winter's Tale* we see Dorcas ask Autolycus "Is it true too think you?".

A lot of the topical ballads were true in the most part, but the facts were coloured by the ideas of the writer. Anyway, a good ballad vendor could convince his public that anything in print was the truth.

The 17th century saw no improvement in the reputation of the ballad seller; a number were found to be in league with cut-purses who worked among the crowds that gathered round the seller. The Long Parliament of Cromwell's day instructed the magistrates in 1649 to flog and imprison ballad sellers and confiscate their stock of sheets. These measures, along with religious and political unrest, led to a gradual decline and later partial collapse of the ballad trade.

With the Restoration of the Monarchy and, in 1695, the expiry of the Licensing Act that broke the monopolistic powers of the Stationers' Company, the broadside ballad began to win back some of its old popularity. The turn of the century saw a gradual change in the printing of the broadside; the old black-letter gothic type was replaced by roman or white-letter type and the lengthy ballads of the previous century started to give way to more shorter metrical ballads influenced by the theatre and pleasure gardens that proved such a popular rendezvous at that period.

The broadside ballad now found itself with a more competitive market of chapbooks and newspapers. A chapbook consisted of a sheet folded in four, eight, twelve or sixteen, making a small uncut booklet of 8, 16, 24 or 32 pages and were sold for a penny or half-penny. These had been printed for some time, mainly in the form of pamphlets on political subjects. They were gradually superseded by the newspaper, leaving the majority of chapbooks to take the role of cheap story books, recounting the old folk tales and romances.

Cheap newspapers began to appear in the early part of the century, daily papers in London increased from one in 1702 to nine in the 1770s. At the beginning of the century distribution was limited to the central areas of the capital, but gradually London papers were distributed by Post Office clerks of the road to all parts of the British Isles.

The first regular newspaper in Essex was printed in Colchester. Called the *Essex Mercury or Colchester Weekly Journal* this began in 1773 and was followed by the *Chelmsford Chronicle* in 1764. These provincial papers drew some of their news content from the London papers. In the country newspapers were a luxury and those who took them usually clubbed together to pay for them, each having the paper for an allotted time.*

These chapbooks and newspapers offered cheap and more substantial reading material to a wider public, filling the gap between broadside ballads and the more expensive bound books.

In the latter part of the century broadside ballads began to be printed outside London, presses being set up in many large towns, helping the broadside ballad to hold its own against books and newspapers. Printers continued to issue the old traditional ballads of the past, adding much fresh material from the many thousands of songs that were written for the new pleasure gardens, like those of Vauxhall and Ranelagh in London. Although ballads could be bought in stationers shops or at the printers, there were still enough hawkers and chapmen chanting and selling their broadsheets in the city streets and country fairs to bring comments like that in the *Grub Street Journal* for February, 1735, and quoted in the *Gentleman's Magazine* for that month:

"The scandalous practice of ballad singing is the bane of all good manners and morals, a nursery for idlers, whores and pickpockets, a school for scandal, smut and debauchery, and ought to be entirely suppressed or reduced under proper restriction. If ballads do not, yet, they ought to come under the Stamp Act, and the law look on ballad singers as vagrants."

After this strong attack on ballad sellers, the writer continues his account, even if a little enthusiastically, of how ballads filtered through the social system of the time:

*See John Carter: A Colchester tailor in **Essex people 1750-1900** A F S Brown.

"This brings to mind the ill conduct of many of our middling gentry who suffer their children particularly their daughters to frequent the kitchen, be familiar with the servants and so learn their manners. One part of their conversation turns upon frightfull stories of witches, apparitions, etc., which serve to keep Miss in their awe and in their interest.

"Her delight in the kitchen conversation increases with her years, now she is flattered, taught to show tricks upon cards and play at Romps, which soon makes her forget her birth and think herself on a level with them. Well, Miss is now out of her hanging sleeves and everyone, especially the footman, tells her how pretty she is. Now ballads and love songs are daily presented her and vouched for truth. One tells how a footman died for love of a young lady and how she was haunted by his ghost and died for grief. Another, how the coachman ran away with his young mistress, took to hedging and ditching and she to knitting and spinning and lived vast happy, and in great plenty, and a third, how a young squire, master's eldest son, fell in love with the chambermaid, married her at the Fleet, was turn'd out of doors, kept an inn, got money as fast as hops, till the old gentleman died suddenly without a will, and then his son got all, kept a coach and made his wife a great lady who bore him twins for 12 years together who all lived to be justices of the peace, etc. By such foolish stories Miss is deluded, sighs, pities and at last loves and so too often undone without remedy. Democritus."

The Times in 1786, some 50 years later, still blamed ballads as a source of decadence:

"It has been asserted that one of the first pieces of benefit of the new police will be to suppress the ballad singers whose loose ditties corrupt the minds and morals of the lower classes of the young people of both sexes."

In Fielding's *Authors Farce* of 1730 we have an inside view of an 18th century bookseller's workroom, where his hacks are busy writing chapbooks and ballads:

"Bookseller - Fie upon it, gentlemen, what not at your pens? Do you consider, Mr Quibble, that it is above a fortnight since your 'letter from a friend in the country' was published. Is it not high time for an answer to come out? At this rate before your answer is printed your letter will be forgot. I love to keep controversy up warm. I have had authors who have writ a pamphlet in the morning and answered it in the afternoon and compromised the matter at night.

"Quibble – Sir, I will be as expeditious as possible."

The ballad seller then collects his wares from the printer and sets out to sell them:

Thence I receive them and then sally
Strait to some market place or alley,
And sitting down judiciously
Begin to sing. The people soon
Gather about to hear the tune,
One stretches out his hand and cries
Come, let me have it, what's the price?
But one poor halfpenny, says I,
And sure you cannot that deny.
Here, take it then says he and throws
The money. Then away he goes
Humming it as he walks along
*Endeavouring to learn the song.**

*The Weekly Register 9 January, 1731.

COPPED

BALLADS OF THE 18th & 19th CENTURIES

A popular form of ballad format at the end of the 18th century was the slip ballad, which were usually $4\frac{1}{2}$ inches x 16 inches with a woodcut at the top. More often than not the verses were idyllic pastoral love songs of the pleasure gardens, although a number were based on actual events.

I have found three slip ballads to open this chapter. The first is a ballad with no imprint, but judging by the title was first performed in the pleasure garden or theatre and is about a robbery that must have occurred some time around the 1770s. The full story is told in G T Crook's *The Complete Newgate Calendar* and is entitled *Lambert Reading. Hackney coachman and leader of a Gang of Robbers executed at Chelmsford 10 August 1775 for Burglary.*

Lambert Reading was the leader of a desperate gang of hackney-coachmen who robbed Copped Hall in Essex not far from Epping. He had a hackney-coachman in confederacy, who waited for him at Stratford. A magistrate of the county happened to pass by the coach and was struck at its being there at an unusual hour of the night, from which circumstance he was induced to observe its number.

Hearing the next day of a robbery at Copped Hall, he wrote to Sir John Fielding of his suspicions and named the coach's number. From this information the thief-takers traced Reading to a house in Brick Lane, where they found him in bed with a woman who passed as his wife.

He was surrounded with pistols, hangers, pick-lock keys, dark lanterns and other apparatus for a housebreaker. He had an opportunity of using some of

these arms in his defence, but was so greatly intim-
idated that he quietly surrendered himself. The
material result of the search was the recovery of the
plate stolen from Copped Hall, found hidden in
Reading's apartment in three sacks.

On evidence to this effect, added to other
corroberating circumstances, he was convicted and
executed.

The other hackney-coachman, whose name was
Chapman and who drove for one Conyers,* was taken
on the day of Reading's trial and, being found guilty
as an accessory, also received sentence of death,
afterwards commuted to transportation.

*Copped Hall was owned by the Conyers family from 1739 to 1869.

Five compleat Ken Crackers:
By Oliver Oddfish, Esqr.
A New Song.
Tune - New Market
Of all the Scamps recorded in Story,
Or ken crackers mind what I lay before ye,
Bold Lambert Reading beats them all,
By the Robbery at Copping Hall.
Fal, lal, lal, lal, ly, do

'Twas Esqr Connyer's he did over,
Near Epping, if the truth I did discover,
Long for the prize he didn't wait,
Three sacks he took well fill'd with plate.

Chapman Esqr Coachman was there too,
And Charly Bond, the things did swear too,
He found the wedge in Lambert's room,
And the Crap at Chelmsford was their doom.

He was fast asleep when the trap did come, Sir,
With Drummer Nan, in his own room, Sir,
In his own Ken, for want of sense,
He thought the Trap had been the Fence.

Three Ken Crackers lent assistance,
At Copping Hall there was no resistance,
Nine load of Pistols Lambert had,
And ten Cutlasses near his Bed.

Charles Reading, he was Lambert's brother,
And Billy Archer, was another,
An old Companion of the first,
They safe cou'd one another trust.

The Robbery in Hanover Street, Sir,
At Lady Moystyn's was compleat, Sir,
Wearing Apparel, Plate likewise
It was a most delicious prize.

After they'd bundled up the treasure,
There came Vexation out of measure,
Had not Will Archer fell asleep,
They'd for Lady Moystyn been too deep.

Young Ken Crackers pray all take warning,
It was at Six o'clock in the morning,
A Glazier's Boy first them espied,
They were took and at the Old Baily try'd.

Condemn'd, cast, and went in a cart, Sir,
And at Tyburn did depart, Sir,
The next affair that I shall bring
Of Phillip Reading now I sing.

Lambert, Charles and Phill were three Brothers,
Consider well ye tender mothers,
Poor Phillip did in Newgate die,
After his heart had many a sigh.

Five lads of Spirit I've display'd, Sir,
Four of them Watchmakers by Trade, Sir,
They did their minds to thieving lend,
O now my song is at an end.

Scamps: highway robbers; **Ken:** house; **Ken Crackers:** housebreakers; **Wedge:** silver, money or plate; **Crap:** gallows; **Drummer:** thief who drugs; **Nan:** a serving maid; **Trap:** trick; **Watchmakers:** thieves who steal watches.

During the Seven Years' War, American War and Napoleonic Wars, Essex was home to a number of military camps. At this period they were only temporary camps under canvas and were known to have been at Warley, Danbury, Lexden Heath and Clacton.

Warley was used as early as 1742 as a camp, where tens of thousands of regular and militia troops were encamped during the summer months. It was visited by Dr Johnson in 1778, when he showed some anxiety about the health of the troops. He wrote on 31st October to a friend:

"When are you to be cantoned in better habitations? The air grows cold and the ground damp; a longer stay in the camp cannot be without danger even if the officers can escape."

In October, 1778, King George III visited the camp to review the troops. Accompanied by Lord Petre, the King inspected the troops and a march past of infantry and artillery. Lord Petre wrote afterwards:

"The line then went through their several firings after which the Light Infantry and Grenadiers, with the Artillery marched immediately through the woods towards Little Warley followed by the whole line in two columns where, as well as manoeuvres of attack and defence were performed with the continued firing of musquetry and cannon to which the situation and variety of the ground were very favourable and afforded much pleasure to the numerous spectators."*

The second of our military ballads is about the camp at Danbury. There is very little information on this camp, but it is thought to have been on Danbury Common, probably around the church as this was a high spot. In the ballad there is a reference to a storm that demolished tents and marquees – this is probably the same storm that wreaked havoc at Warley in October, 1779:

"The most dreadful storm that has been known by the oldest man in the county. Storehouses were blown down, powder and stores being spoilt in the heavy rain; tents and marquees were shattered, including those of the Dukes of Devonshire and Argyle. The hospital at Brook Street similarly suffered and the

OFFICER, EAST ESSEX MILITIA, 1816.

*Essex Units in the War, 1914 - 1919, Vol. 4. J N Burrows

lead was stripped from the roof and flung on to the bowling green; a portion of the Horse and Groom was carried away and a falling leaden spout injured a soldier of the Royal Scots so severely that he died within ten minutes. Twenty Seven men were taken to hospital and damage sustained to the extent of £8,000."

A further interesting fact that this ballad highlights is the practice from 1757 to send militia regiments out of their home counties to lessen the urge for desertion.

The broadside about Warley Camp was printed by John Evans who, along with William Howard, had his press in Long Lane. The Danbury broadside has no imprint.

The New Warley Camp
Sold at 41 Long Lane

Farewell my dearest Polly, I am come to take my leave,
For I am going to Ireland my pay for to receive,
And if you will gang along with me your fortune for to try
Once more we'll go down to Warley Camp to lie.

My daddy and my mammy, they swore they would me kill,
For keeping soldiers company, but I do love them still,
Besides I am with child by you, which thing you can't deny,
So along with you I'll go down to Warley Camp to lie.

Now if you are with child, my love, as I suppose you be,
We'll handle it and dandle it, my wife shall follow me,
The knapsack for to carry that she will ne'er deny,
Once more we'll go down to Warley Camp to lie.

And if it is a female and that perhaps may be,
I'll handle it and dandle it, and let it on my knee,
I'll handle it and dandle it, and never let it cry,
So once more we'll go down to Warley Camp to lie.

The first place that we arriv'd at it was in Warley Park,
And there we pitch'd our tents, my boys, as white as any chalk,
Until such heavy showers came pouring from the sky,
So no more we'll go down to Warley Camp to lie.

The fourth of December, as I've heard many say,
There we struck our tents, my boys, and then march away,
With our noble markees we hang them out to dry,
And no more we'll go down to Warley Camp to lie.

Lancashire Militia in Camp

A Broad as I was walking into the flowery fields,
I heard two lovers talking, from hence not many miles,
The tears ran down her ivory cheeks I heard her sigh and say
The Lancashire militia men are going to march away.

Their route it is for Essex, and what shall we do then,
They are such straight and clever and likely fighting men,
But I will go along with them, no danger will I fear,
My heart is captivated and a light bob is my dear.

We marched out of Chelmsford one evening very soon,
And got to Danbury Camp, my boys, early that afternoon
No mess there was for us set up, we lay on the cold ground,
Until our equipage came up, so then we formed a town.

Our tents they were of canvas, our beds they were of straw,
One blanket for to cover us, the Devil none below,
Our knapsacks for our pillows, we laid under our heads,
So there we took our rest, my boys, all on a strawy bed.

We'd neither house nor harbour to shun us from bad weather,
But close confined twelve in a tent, we lay like logs together
Some times the sun so scorched us we know not what to do,
And other times it rained so hard we was wet thro and thro.

Surely the hardest quarters to us it did appear,
We'd neither bread nor cheese, my boys, not a drop of beer
Nor yet a good kind landlady to smile on us and say,
You've had a bad days watch, my boys, come eat and drink away.

On Tuesday night the storm began, distressed was every man,
It tore our tents to pieces, left us naked on the plain,
Then orders were given out for us to march away,
But it was countermanded until another day.

On the 24th November, we left the stormy plain,
And marched unto Maldon, for barracks once again,
So now farewell to Danbury Camp to it we bid adieu,
And if e'er we go there again our sorrows will renew.

Victorian England saw an upsurge in broadside ballad printing that was to overshadow that of the 16th and 17th centuries. By the mid 1800s the output of the presses was tremendous. When a national event or some horrific murder took the public eye, the presses ran day and nigt to supply the necessary ballad sheets.

All this was possible through the introduction of cheap mechanical printing. More printers began to appear in provincial cities and even small country towns had their own printers, who not only printed posters, handbills, etc., but emulated their London counterparts and produced broadside ballads.

In London the centre of the ballad trade had moved from the City into the Seven Dials area of Covent Garden. Charles Dickens describes this area in his book *Sketches by Boz*.

"Seven Dials! the region of song and poetry - first effusions, and last dying speeches: hallowed by the names of Catnach and of Pitts - names that will entwine themselves with costermongers and barrel-organs, when penny magazines shall have superseded penny yards of song, and capital punishment be unknown! Long rows of broken and patched windows expose plants that may have flourished when 'The Dials' were built, in vessels as dirty as 'The Dials' themselves; and shops for the purchase of rags, bones, old iron, and kitchen-stuff vie in cleanliness with the bird-fanciers and rabbit dealers, which one might fancy so many arks, but for the irresistable conviction that no bird in its proper senses, who was permitted to leave one of them, would ever come back again. Brokers' shops, which would seem to have been established by humane individuals, as refuges for destitute bugs, interspersed with announcements of day-schools, penny theatres, petition-writers, mangles, and music for balls or routs, complete the 'still life' of the subject; and dirty men, filthy women, squalid children, fluttering shuttlecocks, noisy battledores, reeking pipes, bad fruit, more than doubtful oysters, attenuated cats, depressed dogs, and anatomical fowls, are its cheerful accompaniments."

John Pitts, of 14 Great St Andrew's Street, Seven Dials, St Giles-in-the-Fields, started printing in 1802 and appears to have succeeded his 18th century predecessors, taking over their ballad stocks, type and woodcuts.* In 1813 James Catnatch moved his family to a little shop at 2 Monmouth Court, Seven Dials, from Newcastle-upon-Tyne, with an old wooden press and a small assortment of type and woodcuts.↑ His shop is described as 'a little back parlour. In it was an old wooden demy two-pull press, which, when in full work, would raise the floor above it to which the steadying-beams were attached, several inches and would rock the old four-poled bedstead, which stood immediately overhead, like a cradle every time the bar handle was pulled home."

These two printers began to compete for the ballad market and went to great lengths to outdo each other, even circulating lampoons about each other.

Pitts cautioned his ballad writers not to write for Catnatch, but soon they found they could sell their ballads to both houses and then left the two printers to accuse each other of reprinting an early copy, from the other's press.

These two printers between them took the lion's share of the market, though there were others printing in the London area, who we shall meet later.

The broadside ballad of Victorian London was hawked through the streets by what were termed 'running patterers'. This fraternity of ballad sellers worked on the move, crying the titles of the latest ballads that had been rushed off the presses that day. There were also 'standing patterers', who would recite or sing the verses on the sheets that were for sale. In *Chambers Journal* June, 1886, a writer describes another way of selling ballads called a 'pinner-up', "who takes his stand against a dead wall or a long

***John Pitts, Ballad Printer of Seven Dials, London** by Leslie Shepard

↑The Life and Times of James Catnatch, ballad monger by Charles Hindley

range of iron railings and, first festooning it liberally with twine, pins up one or two thousand ballads for public perusal and selection. Time was when this was a good thriving trade and we are old enough to remember the day, when a good half mile of wall fluttered with minstrelsy of war and love under the guardianship of a scattered pile of pinners-up."

The broadside ballad was also hawked round country fairs and markets. Pedlars would carry them in their packs along with needles and pins and other necessities that countrywomen needed. They were pasted up in inn parlours and milkmaids pinned them in the dairy, where they then learnt the latest songs while milking the cows.

Alfred Williams who collected folksongs in the Thames Valley in 1914, writes about the country ballad trade:

" The songs were mainly obtained at the fairs. These were attended by the ballad singers who stood in the market place and sang the new tunes and pieces and at the same time sold the broadsides at a penny each. The most famous ballad singers of the Thames Valley in recent times were a man and woman who travelled together and each of whom had but one eye. They sang at all the local fairs and the man sold the sheets, frequently wetting his thumb with his lips to detach a sheet from the bundle and hand it to a customer in the midst of singing."

The latter part of this account illustrates the thinness of the paper that was used for ballad printing in the 19th century. It was about A4 size and almost like tissue, very fragile and so easily torn or des-troyed; it's a wonder that so many have survived to the present day.

For the ballad singers who travelled the country districts, Essex provided a rich market within easy reach of London. The marshes of the Lea Valley and Epping Forest formed a natural barrier and prevented the massive Victorian speculative building programmes moving very far eastwards. Even today the forest provides a district line between suburbia and rural districts. For the ballad singers then it was within a day's walk from collecting the latest ballads from

Seven Dials, out through the City and across Bow Bridge to Stratford and then fanning out into the rural Essex countryside.

One Essex event, very near London, that attracted all kinds of travelling showmen was the annual fair at Fairlop. This was held on the first Friday in July, under Fairlop Oak, a large tree in Hainault Forest.

The Fair was the outcome of the eccentric activities of Daniel Day, a block and pump maker of Wapping. Mr Day was the proprietor of a small estate not far from the Oak. On the first Friday in July he would go there with a number of neighbours and friends, travelling in a boat on wheels drawn by horses, to collect his rents, ending the day with a feast of beans and bacon.

Daniel Day died on 19th October, 1769, aged 84, and was buried in a coffin made from wood from the Oak.

As time went on, the Fair increased in size until in the early 19th century it lasted from Friday till Sunday, drawing some 60,000 people and sporting theatrical shows, wild beast shows and many gambling and drinking booths.

During Daniel Day's lifetime the boats started from Wapping Old Stairs and Day would join them at Barking Creek after travelling down by water. After his death the Barking route was dropped and the boat was brought direct from the East End through Bow and Stratford.

A description of the procession as it took place in 1840 is recorded in a contemporary periodical:*

"The roads leading to Ilford, and thence to the Fair, presented a scene of animation and bustle from morn to night, with the East-enders proceeding to and from the fair. Vehicles of every description were in requisition, and numberless vans, each drawn by two horses, covered with awnings and gaily decorated followed each other in rapid succession along the Lea Bridge and Mile End roads. Great confusion sometimes prevailed at the turnpike gates from the number of

*The Fairlop Oak and Fairlop Fair by A G Credland. **Essex Journal** Vol. 14, No 3, Winter, 1979/80.

vans, gigs, omnibuses and carts, etc., waiting to pass. The police had an arduous duty to perform at the gates, but they pleased everybody with their mildness and forebearance, and the jokes levelled at them they took in good part. The impositions of some of the turnpike-men were loudly complained of, and they would have been greater but for the attendance of the police.

"The great attraction of the day were those amphibious vehicles, the watermen and blockmakers' boats, mounted on carriages, and each drawn by six post horses, with postillions superbly dressed. The watermen's boat, which is called the *Unity* had been repainted for the occasion, and great pains had been taken in decorating her. She has three masts, and was rigged out exactly like a ship; the sides of the boat were painted a bright yellow, with false posts, and a gilt streak round. The boats, masts and riggings were covered with streamers and flags, and the horses attached to the carriage which supports the boats were decorated with ribbons. The Wapping Watermen, a set of jolly fellows, who prided themselves on a good turn out on this day, were dressed in their best clothes. At half past seven the *Unity* got under weigh, from Green Bank, Wapping; the band who accompanied the watermen playing "God Save the Queen" as she started, amidst the cheers of the spectators. The *Unity* proceeded along in fine style, and being unable to pass under the arches of the Blackwall railway, in consequence of the height of the masts, passed over Old Gravel Lane, Ratcliffe Highway, Upper East Smithfield, the Minories and Whitechapel Road. The wives of the watermen followed in open landaus, and the rear was brought up by a large van, covered with an awning, containing about 50 persons and a band of musicians. The van was drawn by six horses and was very neatly adorned with ribbons, nosegays and colours. In the Mile End Road the procession was joined by the *Maggot*, the blockmakers' boat, also drawn by six grey horses. The masts and rigging of the *Maggot* were decorated similar to the *Unity*, and was followed by open barouches, each drawn by two horses containing the blockmakers' wives.

"The procession was a very imposing one, and attracted a vast number of spectators who lined the roads, their appearance with the flags and banners waving in the breeze was singularly interesting while the music re-echoed through the woods and fields. The watermen remained in the fair about an hour and a half, then proceeded to Chadwell Heath to hold their bean feast. The blockmakers remained in the fair about the same time and then went to Woodford to dine and play at cricket and trap and ball."

A number of ballads were printed about the Fair.

W S Fortney, who inherited the stock from both Pitts and Catnatch presses and reissued many of their best items, printed a ballad called *Don't touch my girl* possibly a localised version of a music hall song. It appears on a sheet of three songs called *Have you seen my Polly?* and recalls the ups and downs of the journey to Fairlop; another in the same vein was printed by Henry Parker Such of 177 Union Street, Borough, S E London, called *Fairlop Fair*

A collection of favourite songs
W S Fortney Printer Monmouth Court London W C
Don't Touch My Girl

About a month ago we went to Fairlop Fair,
Took Sarah for a spree, we looked a nobby pair
We went down in a van me and two or three more
And if I had have counted the kids, there must have been a score,
But Mr Porkey Joe, he thought I must of been a dunce,
He got up to his tricks so I gave him the tip at once.

Keep your mawlers off of Sal,
I don't allow you to touch my girl,
Hit me, smash me, knock me down,
But don't you touch my girl.

As we went along the road didn't we cut it gay,
The horses had their load and a good blow out of hay,
There was plenty of grub in the van, I fell on my pipe,
After having a swig in the can Sal fell off her tripe,
But Mr Porkey Joe couldn't leave Sal alone,
Then I spoke to him again in a sort of undertone.

When we got to the Fair, Sal got into a swing,
Porkey Joe was there doing the highland fling,
We went and brought a pea shooter, such a fizzer made of tin,
And every now and then he'd shove a hot 'un in,
We went down some shady lanes to have a repose,
But Mr Porkey Joe landed a horse bean on Sal's Nose.

The time it passed away, when Joe to me said,
'How is it that you can come and punch my head.'
Before a word I could say, with his left he let fly,
I Bauked it off so nice in the corner of my eye,
Then we formed a ring got it left and right,
Two Peelers coming by locked us up for the night.

Fairlop Fair
Tune Maypole

Last Fairlop Fair to drive away care,
To toddle there we swore,
There was ugly Bob and Sam the snob
And five and twenty more.
Pat Murphy promised fair,
So him we couldn't doubt
And what was pleasant I declare
Our Mothers let us out.   Tol, lol, etc.

A cart and a horse we hired in course
Of costermonger Joe,
Who swore the nag was like a stag,
A regular good'un to go.
We took him at his word
And paid a sovereign down
And away we toddled, toddled, toddled,
And hooked it out of town.

Sam wore whites and Bob wore tights
With a spicy long tailed blue,
While all the rest was up and dressed
In toggery 'patter as new'.
Beside it was agreed
By Sam and ugly Bobby
A nosegay we should wave apiece
To make us all look nobby.

Away we went on pleasure bent,
As hard as we could trot,
The horse looked bold, no wives did scold,
But the sun was werry hot,
The perspiration rolled,
The ladies' colours ran,
Which clearly proved and no mistake,
They'd all been in the sun.

A treat, I'm blowed, was down the road
To see him gallop hard
When all at once, the stupid dunce,
He wouldn't stir a yard,
We guv it him over the nob
And wopped him on the flank,
But, lord, you might as well have tried
To move the precious bank.

The people laughed and jeer'd and chaffed,
As down the road they passed,
Though we be as first sirs, Bob I'm cussed,
If we shan't be the last.
We shov'd away behind
And so did Bob's fat mother,
But as fast as we could shove one way,
The hunter shoved the other.

At last cries Sam, 'I've got a plan.'
Then a bunch of carrots ties
To the end of a stick, an artful trick,
And fixed 'em afore his eyes.
Away the hunter went
With his precious liven load,
When all at once the tail fell down
And spilt us on the road.

The women ball'd, the babies squall'd,
We looked our selves for dead:
Some was hurt and choked with dirt
And some pitched on their head.
The grub got spilt on which
Our hopes did so suspend
And the goosegog pie had all go jamm
By Bobby's latter end.

By the time we'd got quite over our fright,
The folks were coming back,
So we got done out of our fun,
Through the precious lazy hack.
Next time we pleasuring went,
We swore with all our rage,
If we couldn't go by better horses,
We'd go by the Marrowbone stage.

There are two ballads extant printed by Thomas Birt of 10 and 39 Great St Andrew Street, Seven Dials. He issued ballads between 1833 and 1841, after which his business was taken over by his widow, Mary, until 1851, when her son, George, took over. The one I have chosen gives details of the route taken by the boats, the other includes a paragraph on Daniel Day and the Fairlop Oak.

Fairlop Fair
Printed by ---
Wholesale and retail   9 seven dials
Country orders promptly attended to
Every description of printing attended to
A few years before Mr Day died, his favourite oak lost a limb
out of which he procured a coffin to be made for his own
internment and often used to lie down in it to try how it would
fit him. He died in October 13th 1767 aged 84 and his remains
was conveyed to Barking by water, pursuant to his own request
accompanied by six journeymen Block and Pump makers to each
of whom he bequeathed a new leather apron and a guinea.

Come to Fairlop fair, my good fellows, invite
To partake of that day it is our delight,
For we have spirits like fire, our courage is good,
And we meet with the best respected on the road;
Could you see us, you'd say when we are mustered quite gay,
Success to the lads that delight in that day.

Haste away, Haste away, all nature seems gay,
Let's drink to the joys of Fairlop so gay.

Our horses are of the very best blood,
Our boat she's well built and her rigging is good;
With our coats and our badges we unanimous agree,
And join hand to hand to sport the old tree.
With our hearts so delighted our music shall play,
While a pair of staunch ponies shall tow us away.

'Twas one Daniel Day invented this fair,
As harty a fellow as ever was there;
The Lord of the Manor our charter did gain
And we sons of Neptune will hold up the same,
We'll enjoy all the pleasures that spring from that day
And ever remember that old Daniel Day.

From Wapping Old Stairs away then we drive,
Upon the first Friday that comes in July;
We breakfast at Woodford, at Loughton we lunch,
And return back to Rouden's to dine and drink punch;
Then our bootman starts us away to the fair,
While Phoebus does shine on our colours so clear.

It's when from the forest to Ilford we steer,
Every town we go through we give them three cheers;
Then up to Tommy Wright's for there to get refreshed,
Then to return back to Wapping to sup of the best,
Where we will dance and well sing so cheerful and gay
And ever remember that old Daniel Day.

Now having described our boat, horses and crew,
And our Fairlop so gay, which you all do review;
Our boat comes home by the winding of a caul
And now you are welcome unto Fairlop all,
Our boat we'll put by for another Fair day
And ever remember that old Daniel Day.

A ballad sheet printed by P Smith in 1817 gives a description of Fairlop Fair, Daniel Day and the oak, along with some verses. The whole sheet is illustrated by a woodcut drawing showing the Oak and around it a number of beflagged tents. Two three-masted boats are shown arriving, each drawn by six horses. This was printed at Fairlop Fair, so presumably he had a portable press and ran off his ballads on the spot.

As no address is given with the imprint, it may have been the same printer that issued 'The Wicked Woman of Chigwell' and had his shop in High Street, London.

Printed by P Smith at Fairlop Fair July 1817
Fairlop Oak
[detailed description of the Oak, the preservation of the tree, and the Fair's founder, Mr Day]
Song
Sung under Fairlop Tree in the Waterman's Boat
Tune Lady M'Intosh's Fancy

Lads, let us jovial float,
Merry in our tight rigged boat,
Our pilot so gay with badge and coat,
Shall tow us along.
The music shall so sweetly play,
And all shall be so blithe and gay,
We'll laugh and joke,
And drink and smoke,
And join the cheerful song.

Lads, let us jovial float, etc.

On the first Friday, after June,
Like all birds we're in full tune,
We rise up in the morning soon.
Our neat boat for to trim;
From St George's turnpike we do start
And with joy from home we part;
Music playing,
Colours flying,
Then the joy begins.

Lads, let us jovial float, etc.

Then first to Ilford we do steer,
And when we have had breakfast there,
Then to Romford do repair;
*   From thence to Hornchurch go;*
Then back to Romford for to dine
Off English beef with foreign wine,
*   Singing, dancing,*
*   Life enhancing;*
For pleasure all on tiptoe.

Lads, let us jovial float, etc.

Then to Fairlop Fair we steer,
With carriages in front and rear,
Our skins quite brimful of good cheer,
*   So mellow then we start,*
Then we o'er the forest ride,
Neither fearing wind nor tide;
*   Singing, laughing,*
*   Drinking, quaffing,*
Merrily we glide.

Lads, let us jovial float, etc.

When Phoebus to the west draws near,
And the feathered race disappear,
Then from the forest we do steer,
*   To Ilford awhile to stay,*
Then from the Angel to Ilford,
Merry we tow'd along the road,
*   All hearty jovial,*
*   Quite convivial;*
So finish the day.

Lads, let's jovial float, etc.

*A History of Fairlop Fair with songs sung in
the boats* was printed by John Vandenburg Quick of
43 Bowling Green Lane, Clerkenwell, headed by a wood
cut similar to the one used by P Smith and having a
description of the Oak and Fair. There were three
songs on his sheet, two of them reprints from other
sheets. (*Come to Fairlop Fair, good fellow invite* is
titled 'Sung from the Waterman's boat.) His third song is –

FAIRLOP FAIR,

WITH THE SONGS SUNG IN THE BOATS.

Song from the Blockmaker's boat
          sung by
          Mr Hemingway

To George, our late King, as he sat on the throne,
The supporters of Fairlop sent in their petition
That he the old oak in true wisdom would own –
Was the answer return'd from the head of the nation,
So thus we agree that the Maggot and Spot
Ne'er shall be crushed, but for ever shall reign.
          Chorus
A Charter we've got to support the old spot,
So Fairlop shall flourish again and again.

This answer so noble, abroad quickly spread
The enemy to friendship began to complain,
That to this fair mischief was surely the head,
And if suffer'd would certainly soon show its aim,
Down, cried he, with this Fairlop tree,
But George, ever generous, said, cease to complain

Freedom, the Goddess for Britons, so fair,
When she heard that a few supporters so free,
Did rev'rence the oak, which was always her care,
And she said that the day ever sacred should be;
The Maggot and Spot the care of us all shall be,
And ne'er shall be crush'd, but for ever shall reign.

Bright July comes on when we are so gay,
The first Friday in the month, that we all know;
Our Maggot for ages shall shine on that day
And every year some new splendour shall show.
When we agree that the Maggot and Spot,
Ne'er shall be crushed, but for ever shall reign.

Now, my brave boys, since united we be,
With friendship and harmony keep up the day,
Our boat rigg'd and mann'd well, so pleasant to see,
There's nothing can equal our Maggot so gay.
A toast, I say, to good Daniel Day,
Who taught us first this fair to maintain.

A few weeks after Fairlop Fair and only a few miles northward, there was another and much older custom taking place at Dunmow. The origin of the flitch custom is of such great age that it is now lost to us. The custom of giving a flitch of bacon to a couple who were happily married, managed not to quarrel for a year and a day, and could swear an oath to that effect, is not unique to Dunmow, but has counterparts in other English and European towns.

The first mention of the custom at Dunmow was by William Langland in 1362 in his poem *The vision of Piers Plowman.*At this time the flitch was awarded by the Prior of Dunmow Priory; after Henry VIII dissolved the monasteries, the award was given by the Steward of the Manor. Intermittent claims were made up until the 19th century, when the ceremony was revived by the author, William Harrison Ainsworth, in 1855. The couples were given a mock court hearing, with a jury of six bachelors and six spinsters. After the trial the sucessful couples were taken in procession to a field nearby, where the awards were presented and the rest of the day was spent in indulging in rural sports and amusements. With some 7,000 people present there would have been a steady market for the ballad sellers.

By the end of the century the trials were being performed yearly and, as there are a number of different broadside ballads about the Dunmow Flitch still in existence, the custom must have been a good sales line for the country trade, especially in the immediate vicinity of Dunmow.

The earliest broadside ballad about the Flitch was printed by T Evans of 79, Long Lane, who was issuing ballads in the 1790s. The ballad, as far as I can see, is entirely fictitious, but the date seems to suggest that it was probably issued for sale at the time of a very popular ballad opera called *The Flitch of Bacon* by Henry Bate, who later became a parson at Bradwell-juxta-Mare. This opera remained popular from 1778 to, at least, 1786 and was performed at Chelmsford and Norwich as well as at Covent Garden.

The
Spruce Mr Clark
Printed and sold by T Evans 79 Long Lane

The Spruce Mr Clark
Was a young Essex spark,
A farmer luxurious and rich;
He loved dearly as his life,
Fried bacon and his wife;
And, says he – 'My duck, we'll claim the Flitch.'

Mrs Clark ('twas in bed)
Loved bacon, she said,
But she vow'd she'd no more see it spoil'd;
Crying – 'Clark, you're quite mistaken,
If you think to fry that bacon,
I insist every bit shall be boil'd.'

Mr Clark, tho' 'twas night,
Jump'd in bed bold upright,
Quite enragèd at his rib by his side,
And, says he – 'Now madam, mark;
Too, I love you, Mrs Clark,
I'll be damn'd, it shan't all be fried.'

The dispute ran so high,
'Twixt a boil and a fry,
That Clark, tho' he argued it roundly,
Put an end to all turmoiling,
As to frying or to boiling,
By basting Mrs Clark, very soundly.

These turtles, no doubt,
Very soon found out,
That their claim to the Flitch must be shaken,
They had children blythe as larks,
But all the little Clarks
Were mark'd with a rasher of bacon.

There are two ballads referring to the 1855 trial. *Dunmow Flitch of Bacon* contains references to the winning couple, Le Chevalier and Madame de Chatalain.* The other, with the same title, was printed by H Disley, 57 High Street, St Giles, London. Disley, who flourished during the 1860s and 70s, had worked for Jemmy Catnach before setting up on his own. His ballad has a reference to Mr E T Smith, lessee of the Theatre Royal, Drury Lane, who was the organiser of the trial and provided banners, garlands, costumes and other decorations.†

Dunmow Flitch of Bacon

Come all you lads and lasses fair,
And cheer this undertaking,
And with wives lead peaceful lives,
And get the Flitch of Bacon.
This Dunmow is a precious place,
Renouned through England wide O,
And France as well, who strange to tell,
Now claims the Flitch with pride O.

Then cheer up boys for Dunmow's joys,
Your hearts no longer aching,
And never wop your wives again
And feed them well on Bacon.

No more have jars or angry wars
With your kind precious spouses,
And let them do just as they please,
Yes, even wear the trousers;
And all you single chaps and girls
Your marriage vows be taking,
Get all your rhubarb planted in,
And claim the Flitch of Bacon.

---

*Ballad quoted in **The History of the Dunmow Flitch Ceremony** by Francis Steer. No imprint given.
†For text see **Bushes and Briars** D M Occomore.

Give all your money to your wives,
Don't ask them how they've spent it,
For if you do, depend upon't
You surely will repent it;
For in the Union no man now
His wife need now be taking,
But lead a jolly peaceful life,
And live on Dunmow Bacon.

A Frenchman has been bold enough
To try this undertaking,
And all the way from France has come
To claim the Flitch of Bacon.
One twelvemonth long no angry words
Or quarrels have they taken,
And now the French man and his wife
Shall have the British Bacon.

The very hogs for miles around
Now in their styes are quaking
And squeaking to each other cry,
'O damn the Flitch of Bacon.'
For every poor man in the land
No pig's stye need be making,
But lead with wife a peaceful life
And claim the Flitch of Bacon.

So all you Essex wives and maids,
Your sides with laughter shaking,
You all shall have a bustle made
Out of a Flitch of Bacon.
And all you sorry single chaps
In bachelor's situation,
Come to the altar, lead the dears,
And give 'em Dunmow Bacon.

Your children like the olive tree
Shall grow, and soon be taking
To plough and drive, and laughing thrive
On beer and bread and Bacon.
And if your wives bad tempered are,
And airs on them be taking,
You soon will bring them peaceful round
If you just stop their Bacon.

And in conclusion, married men,
In every grade and station,
Get all the children that you can
To beat the Russian nation.
And three cheers for the blessed man
Who raised this undertaking,
His name it shall for ever live
And be engraved on Bacon.

The next ballad is about the 1857 trial.   *Essex Dunmow and Bacon*   [no imprint given] refers to the winner, Mr Thomas Jeremiah Heard of Staffordshire (not Nottingham, as stated in the ballad), who was a policeman.   *Song of the Flitch* was probably printed by W S Fortney, as the woodcut of a portly gentleman that appears on this sheet was used by Fortney to illustrate another of his ballad sheets.

ESSEX
Dunmow and Bacon

You Essex lads and lasses all,
So handsome gay and jolly,
By wind and steam away they go
From country town and city.
There's twenty thousand old and young,
If I am not mistaken,
With a loud Huzza! – this glorious day,
We will claim this flitch of bacon.

Ch   Thus married by love and agree,
*   And if I am not mistaken,*
*   You may next year to Dunmow steer*
*   And claim the flitch of bacon*

Pretty Mary leave her cow,
And off she goes so mellow,
Buxom Jonny leaves his plough
And trips across the meadow,
O'er the stiles and up the lanes,
They will not be mistaken,
For Jonny says to pretty Jane –
"I wish I had the bacon."

There's Dick the snob and Metfield Bob
And pretty Stratford Mary,
So plump and fat in Jack Shepherd hat,
Goes over the fields, so airy
Next week, says she "will married be"
Love shall not be foresaken,
There is nothing beats
A lump of Dunmow Bacon.

A farmer does at Stansted live,
A very rum old joker,
He swore his wife he would well wop,
With shovel and with poker,
They were fighting like dog and cat
And such a row was making,
The old woman said, "Love, I am afraid
You'll never get the bacon."

Now a policeman people say,
One who is a detector
From Nottingham did sneak away,
What a very fine Inspector, .
With his loving wife, so free from strife,
I'm sure I'm not mistaken,
With rolling pin he will sing –
We have gained the flitch of bacon.

The twenty fifth of June the girls in bloom,
From every part will run now,
Huzza! Huzza! this glorious day
We'll see the rigs of Dunmow.
The couples on men's shoulders placed
All through the town are taken,
We will drink and sing, the bells will ring,
Here is Dunmow lads and bacon.

Now as the pretty maids went home
From Dunmow blythe and bonny,
Little Jenny said to Sam,
"I wish that we had married been
I'm sure we would have taken
This glorious day in Dunmow town
The stunning flitch of bacon."

The bells shall ring and we shall sing
The twenty fifth of June now,
And recollect until we die
The glorious flitch of bacon.

Song of the Flitch

Come all you gallant Essex men,
And rally round now pray do.
The flitch is this year claimed again,
By whom I will soon tell you.
For surely 'tis a glorious plan
Your wives to love and cherish,
And he that beats them is no man
And surely ought to perish.

So Essex lads and lasses pray,
Example now be taking,
Be off to church – no longer stay
And claim the flitch of Bacon.

One Jerry Heard – a Suffolk man,
With Sarah for a wife, sirs,
Have lived together on a plan,
Without an angry word, sirs.
For down in Staffordshire they've lived,
Like turtle doves a–cooing
And ever since they've married been,
Have nothing else been doing.

Oh Dunmow is a wondrous place,
With joy the world is shaken,
And thousands come from every town
To see them claim the Bacon.

Policeman Heard from Staffordshire,
Have often thieves been taking,
They now may rest a little while,
For he's come to claim the Bacon.
And though he's taken many up,
Perhaps with staff knocked down too,
He's given his wife but staff of life,
As every man should well do.

THE " ROEBUCK."

THE " BALD-FACED STAG."

So Essex lads where'er you be,
In every rank or station,
Oh with your wives lead peaceful lives,
And you shall all have Bacon.

Another claimant, William Sparke,
Who has his eye on bacon
From silly Suffolk comes as well,
And will the flitch be taking.
He's passed his life in making wheels,
And bodies, too, for coaches,
But never with his loving wife
Had angry reproaches.

The other Jeremy O'Brien
In his claim there's a flaw,
For Mrs B, his poor old gal,
Is just laid in straw.

Francis Steer quotes a few lines from another broadsheet about the 1857 trial, issued by W Dever of 18, Great St Andrew Street, Broadstreet, Bloomsbury, but I have not been able to trace the entire sheet.

The Epping Hunt took place on Easter Monday. The custom was said to have begun in 1226, when Henry III granted the liberty of hunting over this part of the Essex countryside to the citizens of London.

Up until 1853 'mine host' was the landlord of the Bald Faced Stag. When he grew tired or ashamed of the company that the Hunt attracted from London, he handed over to his neighbouring landlord at the Roebuck. Subsequently it was transferred to High Beech, where the publican kept it going until 1882. But in that year and the previous years, the Hunt had become the scene of riot and public nuisance, so it was finally suppressed with the aid of the police. The hunt was described in its heyday:

"At that far-famed spot, brow above Fairmead Bottom, by twelve o'clock there were not less than three thousand merry lieges then and there assembled. It was a beautiful set-out. Fairdames in purple and in pall, reposed in vehicles of all sorts, sizes and conditions, whilst seven or eight hundred mounted members of the hunt wound in and out 'in restless ecstacy', chatting and laughing with the fair. The greensward was covered with ever moving crowds on foot and the pollard oaks which skirt the Bottom on either side were filled with men and boys."

The confusion that resulted after the stag was released led to only a few huntsmen taking part in the chase.

"Meanwhile the stag, followed by the keepers and about six couples of hounds, took away through the covers towards Woodford. Finding himself too near the haunts of his enemy, man, he there turned back, sweeping down the Bottom for a mile or two, and away up the enclosures towards Chingford. Where he was caught nobody knows how, for everybody returned to town, except those who stopped to regale and recount the glorious perils of the day. Thus ended the Easter Hunt of 1826."*

*Greater London, a narrative of its history, its people and its places by Edward Walford.

Matthew's Songster
Printed and sold by J Catnach, 2 Monmouth Court,
7 Dials. Of whom may be had the finest

assortment of Scriptural and Moral Sheets.
In the three kingdoms upwards of One Hundred
Songs set to Music are preparing for publication:
also a great Variety of Halfpenny Books,
Battledores and Lotteries, ornamented with
Beautiful New Engravings, Cards and Handbills
printed Cheap.

EPPING HUNT

All the fun is beginning, broad day is approaching,
All the road now to Epping already is lined,
Some are a gigging it, others are coaching it,
With dust and with smother there's half of them blind
Come, look alive now,
I'm longing to drive now,
If you are ready, why don't.........................
When we're at Epping, you .... can step in,
The Stag or the Horns to get a warm cup.

SPOKEN – Now ostler! ostler! Bring out those horses for those gentlemen; – we've the real good ones, sir. Going to the hunt, sir? Yes, sir, we are – why do you ask? Only because, sir, we sometimes let horses for the Hunt, and then have to hunt for them. I thought you doubted our respectability; although we are not pedestrians, we are well known upon 'Change – my name is Fribble, that is Mr Parthington, and this is Mr Sloejuice. Pray, if I may take the liberty, what colour do you call that horse, it is so very peculiar? Yes, sir, it is what we call very pecooliar; it's a sort of iron-grey, dun, brown, strawberry sort of colour. Has he any fault? None Sir. Why, he looks blind. Aye, that's his misfortune. Now Mr Parthington, there's your horse, and a fine one he is sir, I shall not take your word for it. Why not, sir? Because Lord Kenyon said, that all ostlers were men of straw. Do you know his pedigree? – Yes, sir; he is brother to Agamemnon, got by Alfred out of Saucy Sal, own sister to Blucher out of the famous one-eyed mare. Thank ye for a little deposit sir. Well, how much? We are not very particular, sir – two guineas, we are not very particular; only we likes to have somewhere about the vallie of the hanimal
Oh, all the fun, etc.

Now there's no peace or quiet, for wrangle and riot,
The road is completely in an uproar;
They'll up-set you, and tell you of fate it's the fiat –
I declare such amusement is quite a bore,
Lamp-posts assailing,
Breaking down railing,
Cutting and slashing, and driving away,
'Tis a hundred to one, now, but they pay for their fun, now,
And return home at night cursing the day.

(Spoken) Well, I have almost pulled my arm out, this horse will keep in the middle of the road, how does yours come on, Fribble? Really, I can't hardly say, but he will stop at every public house on the road. My horse seems very dull of comprehension, there, now he has run his head against the errand cart. How does yours turn out? Why he turns out his toes. There! stop again! here's another public house. Oh! father, look here! if here ant old Smudge? old Smudge! What's old Smudge? Why, sir, he was our brewer's collector's horse, sir, he'll stop at every house all down the road; if you wish to get on you must get off. Why, that appears a very odd way to get on. Now then, here's the turnpike – how much? One shilling, sir. Why, it's only sixpence. We always charges double at the Hunt, cause very few ever comes this way back again. Get down, eleven of you in that donkey cart – 'ant you ashamed of yourselves? he never can draw you – yes, he can, cause he has done so seven times afore today. My good man, how would you like it yourself? Why can't say, not being a hass myself. Well, it's surprising how he does it. Why he does it 'cause he is a hass; and though he is a hass, he is not such a hass as to trouble his head about other people's business, cam up.

Oh all the fun, etc.

At twelve the stag is turn'd out in the hollow,
And now the fun of all fun soon begins,
The word's tally ho! my boys, and all follow
When some have long faces, and others broad grins.
There's broken limbs plenty,
Sure nineteen in twenty.
There's scarcely a soul returns well and hearty
The stag's the only one
In this day's good fun,
That is forsooth, unhurt among the party.

(Spoken) Well, here we are at last, ten miles in five hours is not too much speed, I think, for hunters. Coachman, draw your coach a little

further, that the lady may see it all: but don't go any further now, only as soon as the stag is out, let us have eighteen penn'orth as hard as you can go. Well, I'm as hungry as a hunter, now we are at Epping I should like some sausages; waiter, have you any Epping sausages? No, sir, they have not come from London yet, all the real Epping comes from there. It's only the sham ones as goes from here. I say I'll give anybody a shilling to lead my mare out of the pond, she is going to lay down with me, there she goes, you see. Why sir, you and your mare seem to have come out a fishing instead of hunting. Here's the stag in the cart. What have they caught him then! Why I thought they didn't catch him till after the race was over. Oh, I'm down, and it's a mercy my hat saved my head – There they go, yoicks! hallo! I'll give anybody sixpence to catch my horse? Yes. Where! In the pound. With a bit out of his ear? No, sir, with a bit in his mouth. I say, have you seen the stag? What, a great brown thing? Yes. With four legs? Yes. And two great horns? Yes. Well then, I haven't seen him. Do you know where the dogs throw off. I know where the horses throw off, I have lost my horse and can't find him. Never mind, catch another, there's plenty.

Oh, all the fun, etc.

In July, 1856, the Royal Agricultural Show came to Chelmsford, where great preparations were made:

"The town of Chelmsford has done itself honour by the extent and variety of the preparations for receiving and entertaining the Royal Agricultural Society, and its friends. The streets on Tuesday were gay and gorgeous with a profusion of flags and banners of all nations hanging and waving at every possible point. The main entrances to the town, where in olden times the gates would have been, were adorned with triumphal arches of evergreens, and flowers, and even the town conduits and pumps were surrounded by full-grown trees, transplanted bodily. From the windows of the principal buildings and houses hang garlands of laurel-leaves and flowers, and all manner of amicable mottoes were inscribed in full-blown roses of damask red and maiden white.

"The storm of the night refreshed, without much damaging these floral and arboreal trophies, and washed the streets of the neat little town as if in preparation for the crowds of strangers."*
*London Illustrated News 1856.

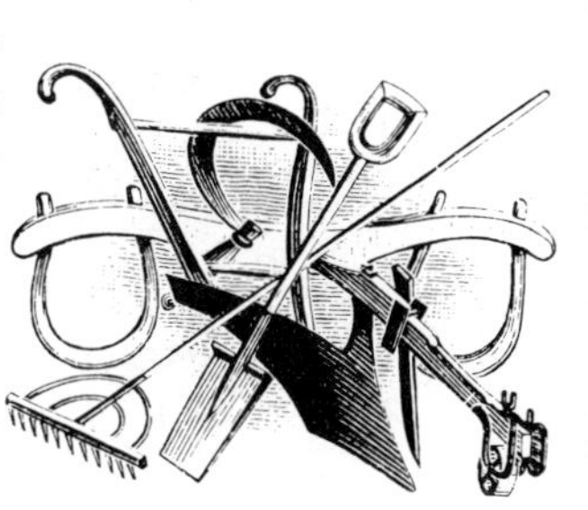

During the week some 2-3,000 visitors attended, to see the trials of field implements and the displays of flowers. The cattle, horse and sheep shows were a sensation.

The *Chelmsford Chronicle* of Friday, 18th July, goes as far as to say:

"The business of this great meeting which will stand as a leading event, we may say will form an epoch in the agricultural history of Essex."

The broadside ballad produced for this event was printed by Dever of 18 Great St Andrew Street, 7 Dials, and has a large VR and royal crest as part of the heading.

Chelmsford Agricultural Show

Come all you jolly farmers that in England do dwell
In Ireland, Wales, Scotland and all foreign parts,
See onward fly in hot July all classes high and low,
To Chelmsford town all to the agricultural show.

From all parts of England, rich and poor in many dresses they go
To Chelmsford for to see the sight of agricultural show,
For miles around they will come in droves to see the grand affair,
Lords and squires, rich and poor, will meet together there.

John to treat his sweetheart, declares he will go,
To Chelmsford for to have a lark at the agricultural show.
It will be seven miles in length, besides the distance round,
It will reach from Chelmsford market place to the back of London town.

There will be porter shops in the corner built, where you may chat and wrangle,
And for to please the married folks a machine to grind them single.
The Queen and Prince Albert, they will come to the show upon the rail,
And old Charley Napier will be there with the blooming Prince of Wales.

In smock frocks and billy cocks the plough boys they will go
The sights to see and have a spree at the agricultural show.
There is ploughs and harrows in gloves and sythes and reap hooks too,
With implements of every kind, how glorious to view.

There is husbandmen of every kind, some that reap and mow,
In jollity will pass the day at the agricultural show.
Oh what would bonny England do! without the lads that plough,
And cause the yellow grain to grow and reap and sow.

Then the pretty little dairy maids with cheeks like a blooming rose,
They will leave the cows and brush away to the agricultural show,
There is shovels, spades and curling tongs, milking pails and wigs
With horses' whips 33 yards long, white nanny goats and pigs.

Where is farmer Chubb, so smart and big, with his great oak stick,
There is farmer Ball and farmer Al, and Mrs farmer Vic.
So you farmers and you husbandmen, your voices raise with me,
May we have abundant harvest throughout this country.

God speed the plough, my motto is, for ever it shall be,
So for Chelmsford agricultural show shout it three times three.
And when the night is over classes home will go,
And tell all the neighbours all about the agricultural show.

Dever, Printer, 18 Great St Andrew Street, 7 Dials

Barking was an important fishing town from the beginning of the 17th century. Defoe wrote in 1722 about Barking:

"... a large market town, but chiefly inhabited by fishermen whose smacks ride in the Thames from whence their fish is sent up to London, to the market at Billingsgate by small boats."

Because of the proximity of the London market and the introduction of the well-boat, where fish could be brought alive and fresh back to port, the Barking fishing industry grew. In 1833 Mr S Hewitt, the largest smack owner at Barking, estimated that there were 120 smacks at Barking, employing some 700/900 men.

The smacks went out generally with supplies for 8 to 10 weeks. Carrying 7 or 8 hands on board, they fished mainly on the Dogger Bank for cod. Barking declined when the railway could bring fish from the east coast ports quickly after being landed by fast steam drifters.

With such a long connection with the sea, it is not surprising that the town of Barking was featured on broadsides. *The Bonny Girl of Barking Town* is a song about a fisherman who leaves his local sweetheart and signs on a ship bound out of the Pool of London for distant ports. This ballad, printed by Marten of Swan Street has a traditional folk song ring to it. The line 'I am going across the briny sea in search of something new' occurs in the song *Adieu my lovely Nancy* that has been collected orally.

The Bonny Girl of Barking Town
Martin Printer 14 Swan Street Minories

Come all you lads of Barking Town, ten thousand times adieu,
I am going to cross the briny Sea, in search of something new,
In search of something new, brave Boys! I brave the stormy wind
I shall ne'er forget old Barking Town and the bonny girl I left behind

I have a loving sweetheart, I must not tell you her name,
Oh how she griev'd to see me start but I refused the same,
The tears ran down her rosy cheeks, but it did not change my mind,
So I said farewell to Barking Town, and the bonny girl I left behind.

I started up to London Town, upon that very Day
Got Shipp'd and signed my articles and drew my one month's pay,
I sported cash till all was gone for so I am inclined
Then bid farewell to my true love the Bonny girl I left behind

Come all you lads of Barking Town, I tell you young and old
You may labour all the Winter, in the stormy wind so cold,
When summer comes the trade falls low as always you will find,
So the raging seas must lure me from the girl I left behind.

'Oh sailor,' said the fair young maid, 'when you away have gone,
I will not wed another as one has lately done.'
A while ago, you well do know, a female proved unkind
She forsook the joys of Barking Town and her bonny laddy left behind

Success to every sailor bold that leaves their native shore,
May they return in safety well blest with gold in store,
For gold it always is your friend as ever you will find,
Success to the jolly young Fisherman and the bonny girl I left behind

Another interesting ballad that has connections with Barking is *The Black Velvet Band*
This has been collected orally in many parts of England and also Ireland. The usual oral version starts more or less the same as that collected from Harry Cox of Catfield, Norfolk:

In a neat little town they call Belfast,
Apprenticed to trade I was bound,
And many an hours sweet happiness
Have I spent in that neat little town.

On the other hand the broadside version issued by the London presses has a more local beginning:

To go in a smack down to Barking,
Where a boy as apprentice I was bound,
Where I spent many hours in comfort and pleasure
In that little town
At length future prospects were blighted,
As soon you may all understand,
So by my downfall take warning,
Beware of a black velvet band.

Barking was also the setting for a dispute over, of all things, manure, causing such a stir that a ballad sheet was issued, probably locally printed, though it may have come from a London press (no imprint). The whole tale is told in the *Barking Record* March, 1975, and I can do no better than quote the story from there:
"Towards the end of the 18th century the largest potato grower in Essex, Mr T Pittman of Barking and Dagenham was using manure from London to augment that from his own yards. The muck from London was not confined to stable manure, but almost every description of animal and vegetable matter, in a state of putrefaction was landed almost daily at the town quay and carted through the town during the

daytime to such great annoyance and discomfort of the inhabitants that following a public petition in 1851 when 200 such cargoes were landed, the landing of night soil was forbidden, the landing of other manure restricted to certain hours and the caulking, careening or burning of vessels banned within 20 yards of the quay, an unexpected riposte to the fishing community many of whom signed the petition. The success of the new regulations may be judged from the following ballad presented to the Valance House Library by Mr H Ward."

BARKING Town *Quay*
New song
Tune   Lord Lovel

The Look Out she lay one fine August morn
Alongside the Barking Town Quay,
When up came a fine manly chap in his trap,
And I think he was styled an M.D. de de.
And I think he was styled an M.D.

What are they about there? the M.D. he said,
What can they be doing? said he.
They are caulking the schooner, the wharfkeeper said,
And are making her tight for the sea, sea, sea.
And are making her tight for the sea.

Oh! they must not do that then, the M.D. he said,
They really must not, Sir! said he;
But, as you're young in office, I'll go and tell them
They are breaking the rules of the Quay, e, e,
They are breaking the rules of the Quay.

But some how or other, the schooner was caulked,
And went on her way to the sea,
When a dung barge that laid near the very same spot
Popped into the berth by the Quay, e, e,
Popped into the berth by the Quay.

They fetched Moggy and Peek and another old chap,
*   Who is called either Joe or Wo ee*
And they whistled and sung and they threw up the dung
*   Right on to the top of the Quay, e, e,*
*   Right on to the top of the Quay.*

Old Wackett then came up and said to old Mog
*   What have you got there, mate? said he.*
Why a dung job, old pal. and it smells rather strong.
*   But is marked, you must know, G.A.B., be, be.*
*   But is marked, you must know, G.A.B.*

The weather was hot, and poor Peeky knocked up,
*   So weary and tired was he;*
So he laid himself down for repose on a log,
But couldn't rest for the louse and the flea, flea, flea,
*   But couldn't rest for the louse and the flea.*

The afternoon came, and old Carpet walked up,
*   To look at what e'er he could see;*
When up came his spouse, and says, "come to your house",
*   For we are all waiting for tea, tea, tea.*
*   For we are all waiting for tea.*

"I shan't come just now", old Carpet he said,
*   "For I don't want none o' your tea",*
So he up with his fist and he gave her a blow,
*   That knocked her flat down on the Quay, e, e,*
*   That knocked her flat down on the Quay*

Next morning Dick Phillips and Co. played their parts,
*   As busy as ever could be,*
And they loaded their filth into several carts,
*   To take it away from the Quay, e, e,*
*   To take it away from the Quay.*

Then up rode a man astride a brown horse,
*   With gaiters near up to his knee,*
To see that the filth was not dropp'd thro' the streets,
*   To endanger the mark G.A.B., be, be,*
*   To endanger the mark G.A.B.*

The M.D. soon after arrived in his trap,
*   And had a short ride round the Quay,*
And believe me – he neither could see nor could smell,
*   Because of the mark G.A.B., be, be,*
*   Because of the mark G.A.B.*

Then out came a chap with a square paper cap,
*   And bustled about on the Quay;*
Says he, "I can't stand it – here boy and go fetch
*   That stout old chap, called Loo Corslee, lee, lee.*
*   That stout chap, called Loo Corslee."*

"It's no use to go there", the boy he then said,
*   "He isn't at home sir", said he.*
"How is that?" said the chap with the square paper cap.
*   "'Cos the dung, sir, is marked 'G.A.B.', be, be,*
*   "'Cos the dung, sir, is marked 'G.A.B.'"*

"Look there!" says a fisher boy, standing close by;
*   "What is that there, old pal? I can see?"*
"'Tis a dummy great dog, with the leg of a hog
*   He's just dragged from the dung on the Quay, e, e,*
*   He's just dragged from the dung on the Quay."*

Then up steps the chap with the square paper cap;
*   "That accounts for the stink, boy", said he*
And two or three others then came round about,
*   And such a sight there they did see, see, see*
*   And such a sight there they did see.*

So they made up their minds, and did say, one and all,
*   The best thing to be done then would be,*
To write to the Metropolitan Board,
*   And ask them to cleanse our Town Quay, e, e,*
*   And ask them to cleanse our Town Quay.*

NOTES
John Manley [verses 1 – 3, etc.] is described in the
Census Returns of 1851 as 'General Practitioner, M.D.
of Edinburgh. Member of the College of Surgeons of
London and Dublin, and Apothecaries' Hall, London.'

He had been born in 1799 in Topsham, Devon, a seaport at one time of considerable importance, but had married a Barking girl and their son, William, 'a merchant', was born in Barking in 1831. The Manleys lived at Westbury House, Barking.

The Wackett family [verse 6] were farmers and market gardeners in Ilford and Marks Gate; and 'G.A.B.' must be George Augustus Burrell, farmer, corn dealer and coal merchant, of North Street and Tanner Street. Elected Surveyor of Highways, 1854 - 67, and Churchwarden, 1859 - 67, George lived with his mother in Ilford Lane and, although he had been born in Romford in 1811 and his mother came from Chelmsford, both his father and great-grandmother lay buried in the churchyard at St Margaret's, Barking.

The Horsleys were another old Barking family, and a Luke Horsley was buried in the Parish churchyard in 1734. The Luke Horsley of verse 13 lived near the Quay, in Fisher Street. Described as a smack-owner, mast, block and pump maker in 1848, by 1851 he had turned his hand to victualling, at *The Still* in Fisher Street.

The Metropolitan Board of Works [verse 17] was elected by the parish vestries and provided London's first central administration, from 1855 until replaced by the London County Council in 1888.

Our next ballad has been speculatively associated with the actress Mrs Dorothea Jordan (1762-1816), mistress to the Duke of Clarence.* James Catnach, who printed it, only arrived in London between 1813 and 1814 and so would, I think, have been too late to cash in on any scandal between Mrs Jordan and the Duke. To me the ballad rings of the early music hall songs like those popularised by Sam Cowell.

*Later English Broadside Ballads, Vol. 2, John Holloway and Joan Black.

Old Woman of Rumford
J Catnach Printer 2 - 3 Monmouth Court 7 dials

There was an old woman of Rumford
And she was a gay old lass,
And many an honest penny got
By selling asparagrass
As through the streets she goes,
With her barrow as she'd pass,
Soliciting her customers
To buy her precious Ar
tichokes and Colliflowers,
Come buy, come buy of me,
They are the finest of the sort
That ever you did see

This old woman had a daughter
And the girl her name was Ciss,
And she went into the garden,
Every morning for to pick
Some parsley, time and sage,
Likewise some asparagrass
To decorate her barrow,
Then she cried come buy my Ar

The old woman had a lodger too
Who used to bed and board,
She resolved one morning to treat him with,
A good brown roasted turkey,
She boiled some colliflowers
Likewise some asparagrass,
For she made a lovely HITT,
And sold her precious Ar

This put the lodger in a rage,
Said he, 'my cunning old lass,
If you give me further impertinence,
I'll kick your precious Ar
tichokes and tender flowers
From your barrow as you pass.'
Oh no, you must not touch me,
Nor my daughter's precious Ar

But if you'll wed my daughter Ciss
Five hundred pounds I will pay down,
Which I've got by my grass,
Then she may be a lady gay,
Visit opera, ball or farce,
And never mind what people say
About her old mother's Ar

This was not to be resisted,
So he pocketed the cash,
And not being close fisted,
Resolved to cut a dash;
He had parties every day to dine,
Made each guest fill up his glass,
And the first toast he gave in a bumper,
'Here's success to the old woman's Ar

An offshoot of the broadside market is explained in P M Handover's book *Printing in London*

"One line was well established in the course of the century, certain petty officials and tradesmen began to send their 'Worthy Masters and Mistresses' reminders that a Christmas box should be forthcoming. One London firm who specialised in this trade, Reynells, claimed that they started their series for beadles and bellmen in 1735 and they were still printing the appeal of the beadles and the sub-inspectors of nuisances in 1879.

The appeal was a simple sheet printed on one side, but by the 1790s the size was impressive, about 21" x 17". The increased size of sheet being used by newspapers had been taken up by the jobbing printers. At the head was a block representing the beadle and bellman passing through the parish, with frames trumpeting their progress. The frame was completed with roughly-cut blocks illustrating up to eighteen episodes from the life of Christ. Below the heading block was the name of the parish of the beadle making the appeal. The interior of the sheet was filled with verses which were varied from year to year on a permutation system. These verses were rhetorical addresses to a great range of persons and subjects. In 1830 the cost of these sheets to the beadle was 200 or more at 5s.6d. a 100, for 100 only 6s. He could hardly have failed to show a profit on this investment and so no doubt did the printer, repeating many of the blocks and many of the verses for over 30 years."

One William Mead, who was bellman of West Ham, issued his verses entitled *A Copy of Verses humbly presented to all my worthy masters and mistresses in the Parish of West Ham in the County of Essex by William Mead Bellman and Cryer.*

These were printed in the usual manner as described above, by S Bayley, 120 Petticoat Lane, White chapel for the year 1800, "Where Catalogues, Hand-bills, Club orders, Tradesmen's cards and Shopbills, etc. are neatly printed at most reasonable rates and on the shortest notice."

The sheet is probably of a stock variety with the Bellman's name and Parish printed in to order. Headed by a wood engraving of the Bellman and his dog supported each side by angels with trumpets. The sides and bottom of the sheet have 18 small Biblical pictures depicting the life of Christ from birth to ascension. The centre is divided into three columns of verse, starting with a

Prologue

Encourag'd by the favours of last year,
Your bellman once again a poet here
Or rather doth assume the poet's name,
Without his genius or poetic flame,
But patrons gen'rous, as a proverb says
Will kindly deign to read these humble lays,
And though much wit they boast not to impart,
They'll speak the honest dictates of his heart

Then follow verses on the saints, Christmas eve, Christmas day, New Year day, twelfth night, the King and Queen. To Masters, Mistresses, young men and maids, finishing with the Bellman's prayer and the

Epilogue

If aught can merit in these artless lays,
Your Bellman humbly thanks you for your praise,
When he at first began to rhyme
It was in consequence of Christmas time
Hoping that from your bounty he might fare
The better at this season of the year,
Meanwhile accept these lines in friendly part,
The honest meanings of a grateful heart.

In 1834 the Poor Law Amendment Act was introduced to try to reorganise existing methods of poor relief. Under this Act many new workhouses were built, supervised by Boards of Guardians. They were responsible for a group of Parishes known as Unions. Many of these workhouses were grim establishments with harsh discipline, little comfort, sparse food. Familes were split, men in one part and women in another, wearing what amounted to a prison uniform. The idea of this system was to deter all those but the desperate from applying for relief.
The ballad *Essex and Liberty* printed by W Taylor is calling for the support of Essex voters in abolishing this system.

Essex and Liberty
Printed by W Taylor, 14 Waterloo-road, New Cut, Lambeth

Come all you gallant Essex blades,
Of high and low degree,
Attention give with one accord,
And listen unto me.
The election is drawing on apace
Then mind all tyrants' rigs,
And don't be foolish led astray
By Tories, knaves or Whigs.

Chorus:
Unfold the Flag of Liberty,
And to the Commons send
To gain your rights you Essex blades,
Brave independent men!

To repeal the cursed Poor Law Bill,
That on you has the sway,
To find all classes labouring,
And give them honest pay
To vote against taxation,
All pensions, power and place
Those are the men you Essex blades,
To free you all from disgrace.

Base tyranny for many years
Has kept the poor man down,
And though he works like any slave,
The rich will on him frown.
The rich can ride in splendour,
While starving is the small,
The poor man does the labour
And has got to pay for all.

May Barking, Dagnum, Raynham,
Aveleigh, Poorfleet and Grays,
Brentwood, Ingastone and Rumford,
Shew their enemies some play,
Wittom, Colchester and Chelmsford
Ongar and Writtle too.
With Coggeshell and Braintree,
Like men their duty do.

May Horndon, Billericay,
Malden and Dunmore,
Stand up like gallant heroes,
When they to the poll do go
May they soon oppression conquer,
Like Britons staunch and bold,
And may they for their children,
Retrieve the days of old.

The lads of Essex alway did,
Prove loyal, staunch and true,
Then unfold the flag of Liberty,
The banners of true blue
And to obtain your freedom,
Endeavour with all might,
And elect the men who will maintain,
Your liberty and right.

Then fill the glass and let it pass
And drink with three times three,
To the gallant boys of Essex,
Who will fight for liberty.
                                    S Morgan

As a footnote to this ballad there appears the following paragraph in the *Chelmsford Chronicle* on 7 November, 1834:*

"Two men were on the 29th ult. apprehended in Sculcoats, singing and vending a ludicrous and inflammatory burlesque upon the New Poor Law Bill, on the following day their stock-in-trade was burnt by order of the Magistrates, and they were discharged on promising never to do the like again - *Hull Advertiser*

(Two vagabonds were vending the same inflammatory papers in this county during last week. We trust the authorities will look to them. Ed.)"

Between the years 1750 and 1850 over six million acres of the cultivated acreage in Britain was converted from open fields, common land, meadow or waste into private fields.

These enclosures meant that many agricultural labourers who had had the right of keeping cattle or sheep on waste or common land lost this small income that augmented their wages.

In a word, the farmhand became essentially a casual labourer hired and dismissed at will, and lacking even the guarantee as he set out in the morning to work, that he would return with any earnings. The

***News from the English Countryside, 1750 - 1850** Clifford Morsley.

decline of payment in kind reduced him, except at
harvest-time when every hand was needed, to nothing
but a precarious cash wage, which might just cover his
modest subsistence costs. The end of the Napoleonic
Wars flooded the market with discharged soldiers, the
effect of which was reflected in lower wages. Even
though food prices dropped, there were still years of
scarcity and dear bread.

By 1830 farming was becoming mechanised and
the thrashing machine was seen as a threat to winter
employment, as men who could not work outdoors
were employed thrashing corn with flails in the barn.

The poor harvests of 1828 and 1829 did not give
much hope to the agricultural labourer facing another
winter of cold, hunger and unemployment. In the
autumn of 1830 the labourers started to demand higher
and better employment conditions. The first outbreaks
of rioting took place in east Kent, spreading westward
and into East Anglia. There did not seem to be any
central organisation to the riots, though a mystical
figure called Captain Swing evolved, who signed the
various written demands.

The Essex riots were preceeded by a fire at
Rayleigh on 5th November, 1830, started by John
Ewen, whose trial was reported in *The Times* of 13th
December:

"The Rayleigh Fire – The trial of John Ewen,
labourer, 34 years of age, for setting fire to a barn
and several stacks, the property of Mr Sach, at Rayleigh on the 5th of November, came on at Chelmsford
on Friday, and concluded at six o'clock in the evening,
when the jury after deliberating about 20 minutes,
returned a verdict of guilty. Mr Justice Taunton
immediately passed sentence of death upon the
prisoner, and told him he must expect no mercy in
this world.*

James Catnach issued a broadside with details of
this and four other trials under the title of:

*The Times Index 1830. Execution 27 Dec; Trial 13 Dec [also
gives details of Tomas Bateman, mentioned in the following
ballad].

*Trials and Executions of the Rick Burners in
different parts of England
J Catnach 2 Monmouth-court 7 Dials
Execution of James Ewen at Chelmsford on Friday
December 24 for Arson*

*James Ewen was indicted for having maliciously and
wilfully set fire to the barn and stack of Mr Such
a farmer residing at Rayleigh in the County
of Essex.
After a trial of great length the judge summed up
most impartially and the Jury found the prisoner
Guilty. Death. He was executed along with
Tomas Bateman who was convicted at the same
Assize of highway robbery accompanied with
circumstances of savage barbarity.*

A Copy of the verses

*Oh what a dismal sight of woe and wretched misery,
To see so many youths expire upon the fatal tree,
What cries and lamentations, what bitter groans we hear,
Are heard on every side, all from their friends and kindred dear.*

*Ill fated youths, how could you that all laws divine defy.
The precious food which God had sent you basely did destroy,
What pleasure could it yield to see, the farmer's little store
Consumed by devouring flames which he may long deplore*

*How often in the dead of night all in the winter's drear,
The affrighted husbandman asleep not dreading danger near,
Has been aroused from his bed with sorry heat to see
His stack yard wrapped in flames and be reduced to beggary*

*How many a tender mother with bleeding heart may mourn
The loss of her dear son, who thus has died a death of scorn,
Two blooming youths, two brothers dear, along with many more,
Have left their broken hearted friends their downfall to deplore.*

*Heaven grant that soon the time may mend and wages may increase
And working men may with cheerfull hearts may spend their days in peace
When fractious knives in fetters bound and branded with distain,
Shall silenced be then we may see good times return again.*

In Essex riots took place in the north-west corner spreading down through Sheering and Harlow, with the final outbreak at Finchingfield. A second area around Colchester saw more violent action. After a meeting calling for an increase in wages on Mile End Heath, near Colchester, the riot spread east with wide spread destruction of thrashing machines at Ramsey, Walton-le-Soken, Little and Great Clacton on 7th and 8th December.* A local ballad sheet was issued about the Little Clacton Riot and is included in the next chapter on local ballads.

The most profitable broadsides were those about murders, along with the last dying speeches, confessions and lamentations of the murderer:

"His choicest plots or grounds to work upon are drawn most commonly from thieves and murderers, or such notorious malefactors, as puts him in great hope to purchase forty pence.

"The idle wife is inforsted to trust him weekly and that without all hope of having ought, unless some ballad chance to be composed upon some dismal or doleful accident as may be sung to the tune of Well a day. If anything happen to help besides, it must accrew from the next session provided there be some to travel, westward, on whom his is to make that recantation as if himself were the theme he writes. No massacre or murder comes too amiss but brings sufficient matter for invention, wherein he shows himself so nimble."†

So have been described the writers of this type of ballad.

Our county provided a number of murder cases that found their way on to broadside ballad sheets.

Henry Mayhew, in his compilation of street interviews *London Labour and the London poor* spoke to a running patterer who had been in the trade 'upwards twenty years'. Starting at 16 with 'the Last Dying Speech and Full Confession of William Corder', down at Bury St Edmunds, where he was executed and 'got a hat full of halfpence', the sheets were sold by just shouting the important words, "Murder, Horrible,

Captain Swing E J Holsbaun and George Rude
†*The Gentleman's Magazine* September, 1784

Barbarous, Love, Mysterious Former Crimes" without announcing any particulars unless the criminal was well known, then the name was given distinctly.

The running patterer goes on to relate:

"There's nothing beats a stunning good murder, after all. Why! there was Rush, I lived on him for a month or more, when I commenced with Rush I was fourteen shillings in debt for rent and in less than fourteen days, I astonished the wise men in the east, by paying my landlord all I owed him.

"I call my clothes after them. I earn money by, to buy them with. My shoes I call Pope Pius, my trousers and braces, Calcraft, my waistcoat and shirt, Jack Denny, and my coat, Love letters. A man must show some sense of gratitude in the best way he can."

Mayhew's informer tells how he travelled in Essex selling ballad sheets:

"Then Calcraft was pretty tidy browns. He was up for starving his mother – and what better can you expect of a hangman? Me and my mate worked him down at Hatfield in Essex where his mother lives. It's his nature, I believe. We sold her one, she's a limping old lady. I saw the people look at her, and they told me afterwards who she was. "How much?" says she. "A penny, marm," say I. "Serve him right", says she."

There were plenty of lean periods in this type of trade and so the patterer would resort to fictitious crimes. These are called cocks (so-called because they were a good 'cock crow').

Mayhew's informant continues:

"The most popular was the murder at Chigwell Row. That's a trump to this present day. Why, I'd go out, sir, with a dozen of Chigwell Row's, and earn my supper in half an hour off of 'em."

The exact ballad he referred to is unknown, but there is a ballad in St Bride's Printing Library by Pitts called:

A full and Particular Account of a most Dreadful Murder committed by a young lady.

In this ballad a Miss Guard, who was jilted by Mr James Lawless, takes revenge. I have not been able to substantiate the facts as true, so it could well have been the Chigwell Row ballad referred to:

With surprise we have learned that the neighbourhood of Chigwell Row was amazingly alarmed on Friday last, by a crowd of people, carrying the body of Mr James Lawless, to a doctor, while streams of blood besmeared the way in such a manner that Cries of Murder reechoed the sound of numerous voices. It appears that the cause of the alarm, originiated through a courtship attended with a solemn promise of marriage, between him and Miss Lucy Guard a handsome young lady of refined feelings, with the intercourse of a superior enlightened mind who lived with her aunt, who spared neither pain nor cost to improve the talents of Miss G those seven years since the death of her mother in Ludgate Hill, London, and bore a most excellent character untill she got entangled by the deluding allurements of Mr L, who after they mutually agreed and appointed the nuptial day, not only violated his promise (on account of her fortune being small), but boasted through the neighbourhood of the unbecoming manner he had triumphed over her virtue, and treated her with the most degrading contempt (which left her in a languishing situation these six months past), while he chanted his eloquence to another young lady of a stamp more adequately to a covetous mind, namely of great fortune, who took such a deep impression in his heart, that he advanced the most energetic gallantry and obtained her consent, got the banns Published in London, and on the point of getting married to her with a raptorous prospect of holding a rural wedding, yet we find that the intended Bride learned that Miss Guard held

certain promissory letters of his and that she was determined to enter an action against him for a breach of promise, which moved clouded Eclipse over the extacy of the variable Mr Lawless, who knew that Miss G had letters of his sufficient to substantiate her claim in court.

However, he determined to remove that obstacle at all events, which was not only likely to diminish the only Idol which the twofold miser so faithfully worshipped (namely Gold) but was likely to prevent his intended wedding, yet it appears when he comes to traverse his imagination that two unexpected obstacles embarrassed his haughty intellects, first he found himself deficient of legal means to accomplish his desires, and secondly deprived of power, which ambition promoted him to imagine that he should not be vanquished in any aim whatever as he was a wealthy Farmer's Son and nominally termed as a young Merchant on account of the manner he increased his store, while acting as an extensive Factor, for many years a miserable stingy dealer in provisions in general, in which often protected him (as a Hero of Seduction) in various outrageous, while presumptive ostentation rendered him an emblem of terror throughout the London Markets, which urged him to apply to the following stratagems namely to obtain his (precious Love) letters by arbitrary power, while he slily watched and found opportunity, when Miss Guard was lonely at home he came (like a devouring Tyrant) and demanded his letters at the peril of her life, while Miss G as a distinguished young lady, prepared herself with unequal fortitude, and after stating to him the consequence of his unmanly conduct, she cautiously ordered him to quit the premises where to confirm his ambition (which crowned his reward) he readily attempted to get at her trunk which a sturdy scuffle ensued and while she screamed for assistance, he attempted to commit an outrageous violation on her person where to protect her virtue she drew a large carving knife and stabbed him under the leaft breast (which promptly brought him to subjection), when his vehment cries alarmed the neighbours who came to her assistance and found them both in contest at the door while she thrusted him out in a gore of blood which exhibited a scene of such momentary confusion that the most anxious conjecture was unable to draw the slightest idea on the wanton provocation yet it appears through the skilful physicians succeeded in stopping the blood, that they can form but little hope of his recovery, as they are doubted that the knife penetrated an artery (and should it be the case they are decidely of opinion that the wound will put a certain period to his existence) which leaves the indended bride to bewail her disappointment while the valiant Victress was forced to submit judicial decorum in the 19th year of her age where sufficient sponsors voluntary offered to join her recognisance, to await the issue, and the whole of the evidence bound to appear on her Final Trial (which will gratify the curious) where we expect the Wigs at equity will give an electrical oration on amorous gallantry, passionate affection,

breaches of promise, etc., when (Cupid's private Embassadors' of) the precious Love letters, will appear unmasked at Chelmsford ensuing Assizes. Epping Telegraph.
Pitts Printer, Toy and Marble Warehouse
6 St Andrew Street 7 Dials

How cruel Letters moved their love,
Such murder, grief and woe
The roads besmeared with crimson blood,
In streams at Chigwell Row,
Where thousands came with deep surprise
To hear in deep deplore,
A stingy Merchant's dying groan
A bleeding in his gore

A courting to a Lady fair,
This Merchant often went,
Where many a vow of love he made,
And many a letter sent,
But when she gave consent to wed
He flew from her with scorn,
For the sake of gold, so we are told,
He left her there to mourn.

To another maid of fortune great,
This haughty Miser fled,
And for the gold she had in store,
This maid he meant to wed,
While the Lady fair he left to moan,
With grief she often said,
"His letter in a Court would prove
The marriage vows he made!"

At length the intended Bride was told
How this fair Lady meant
To make the Miser's gold in court
His promise to repent,
The intended Bride a vow she made
What ever would her betide,
Until he got his letters back,
She ne'er would be his bride.

While in a Maze the Miser thought,
He'd try both art and skill,
To lose his bride with all her gold
Was sore against his will.
To please the intended bride he swore
His letters he'd obtain
To end the strife he'd lose his life,
Or have them back again.

Then with deceit and force he went
To rob this lady fair,
While all alone aloud she cry'd
For mercy was her prayer,
While like a tyrant raving mad,
Unmodestly he tore,
His valiant Lady drew a knife
And left him in his gore.

Thro' her dismal cries, the neighbours
Where many a tear was shed,
While at the door in a gore of blood,
The hero he lay half dead
Then to a doctor he was brought,
Most shocking to behold,
O see him dying in his gore,
Would make your blood run cold.

When this siege of love this lady
To Justice to relate,
Where many joined her in a bond,
Her Trial to await,
For love and murder she was bound,
At Chelmsford to be tried,
While the misers rave in sorrow,
[He leaves] the intended bride.   *(bad print on this line)*

Another ballad at St Bride's was printed by S G Shaw, printer and bookbinder, Hitchin, and is about the murder of Thomas Lowe and his family by a gang of gypsies. How much truth there is in this sheet is questionable. Printed in Hertfordshire, some good distance from the scene of the crime.

A

Horrid, Barbarous, and Cruel Murder Committed on the Body of Thomas Lowe, his wife, Two Children, and his aged Mother, at Bassington, in the County of Essex, on Sunday night last, the apprehension, and commitment of the Murderers.

The following is an account of a horrible murder, committed a few nights ago in the little hamlet of Bassington in the County of Essex. A poor labouring man of the name of Lowe, had for a number of years inhabited a small cottage about the distance of a quarter of a mile of the above mentioned place. By his diligence and industry he was enabled to support a wife and two children, together with an aged Mother in a comfortable manner and was much respected by his employers and all who knew him. On Monday morning last two of his fellow workmen called at his cottage as they went to work, to get a pickaxe, one of them had left there the Saturday night before. They knocked for some time without receiving any answer, at length they forced the door open, and beheld with astonishment an old mastiff, lying in the passage with his head beat in pieces, but what words can express their horror, when, on entering the apartment they beheld Lowe lying on the floor, his brains beat out, and a large wound in his side, they had scarecely removed their eyes from this dreadful sight, when another more horrible presented itself. In an open bed in a corner of the room lay Mrs Lowe, her throat cut from ear to ear and an infant on her bosom butchered in the same barbarous manner. To complete this horrible tragedy, the aged mother of Lowe, who slept in another bed in the same apartment with another child two years of age shared the same fate, the old woman's head was beat in such a manner that one feature of her face could not be discerned. The neighbouring country was soon informed of this atrocious and bloody deed, Constables were dispatched in every quarter, and we are happy to say that the murderers were discovered the same afternoon they are three well known desperate characters belonging to a gang of gypsies, Lowe's watch was found upon one of them. Lowe had recently received about thirty pounds which was left him by a deceased relation, to gain possession of which, no doubt, was the cause of these monsters perpetrating this bloody deed. They are all three committed to the county jail.

*Stop, passenger, before you go
And listen to this tale of woe,
And from your eyes 'twill draw the tear
When you the same shall come to hear*

*Near Chelmsford, as you must know,
There lived a man called Thomas Lowe,
He had a wife and two children dear,
And an aged mother as you shall hear.*

*Last Sunday night this family,
All sleeping in their beds did lie,
When in three villains came straightway,
And took their harmless lives away*

*They knocked the mother's brains out quite,
All in her tender husband's sight,
The husband then they slew likewise,
In spite of all their piercing cries.*

*The little smiling babe did rest
Asleep upon its mother's breast,
These monsters then, most sad to hear,
Did cut its throat from ear to ear*

*Another child two years of age,
Did not escape these monsters' rage,
Nor yet the aged mother dear,
Though she was in her seventieth year.*

*But now good people, you must know,
That these inhuman monsters now
Are close confined in prison strong,
And will be tried before its long.*

Our next ballad is found in Charles Hindley's
Curiosities of Street Literature and is about the
adventures of the Chigwell Station master's wife and
Doctor Saunders. I have not been able to find any
information about the events in this ballad, but it
seems that the station referred to was on the $11\frac{1}{2}$
mile Ongar extension of the Great Eastern Railway
that was opened in 1864 (now Central Line, LRT). The
Station, now named Debden, was originally Chigwell
Lane.*

The Wicked Woman of Chigwell

Come, one and all, and listen to
This funny little song,
Concerning Mrs Harrison,
I will not keep you long;
She in Chigwell Road resided,
With her husband, so its said,
She swore that Saunders on the 12th of March,
Assaulted her in bed.

So listen to this funny tale,
She tried to cause much strife,
Did this false screaming woman,
The Chigwell Station master's wife.

At Epping sessions, there this case occurred
And she said, now only think,
That the doctor Mr Saunders,
With her played at tiddly-wink;
That he went into her chamber,
When her husband left the room,
How far the story there was true,
I'll let you know full soon.

*Chigwell Station on the Central Line branch to Hainault was
not opened until 1903 and too late for this broadside ballad,
Hindley's book being published in 1871 (see **Railway Magazine**
September, 1968).

She refused to say one word about
Her former course of life;
Oh, is she not a beauty,
This Chigwell Station master's wife
Then the council for the Doctor,
Soon put this lady down,
By asking her the manner
She lived in Peterborough town.

Now a witness he was called,
And when he did pop in;
Pray do you know this gentleman?
She cried, yes, all serene;
But whether it is true or not,
At least the folks do say,
That he with this famed Mrs Harrison
Some funny games did play.

Round Ilford and round Epping,
And Romford too it seems,
That she was very fond of Pork,
And she dearly loved her greens,
But to swear that Doctor Saunders
Assaulted her, 'twixt me and you,
She must tell it to the devil,
For with us that tale won't do.

One word for Doctor Saunders,
That kind and skilful man,
She ought to be well bonneted,
And put in the prison van,
Such disgraceful dirty conduct,
It really was too bad,
And when the Doctor was discharged,
The people were right glad.

Smith, printer, High Street, London

The full horrors of the British law come to light in two ballads printed in Bristol. I again failed to uncover the events surrounding the ballads, but they do not sound like 'cocks', as the people, places and events are too well described.

A full and true account of the execution and sorrowful lamentation of John Moore aged only 15 Who underwent the awful sentence of the Law on Friday last at Chelmsford for robbing his masters house of £270 and setting fire to the same, submitted to the public in a Copy of Verses written by the unfortunate youth to his father and mother the day before his execution and delivered to a friend on the Gallows

From Prison these verses I send,
I was sentenc'd to die, when these verses I penn'd,
So pray all you young people a warning do take,
From my situation and evil forsake.

How early in life did my follies begin,
Tho' only fifteen what a state I am in,
Doom'd in sorrow to lie in this gloomy place,
And tomorrow must die in the greatest disgrace.

A good education my parents bestowed,
With hopes that thro' life 'twould be for my good,
But alas! the sad dawn of tomorrow will prove,
That I slighted their kindness attention and love.

At eleven years old my follies begun,
To my wicked companions with pleasure I ran,
To go with them gambling I fully was bent,
And in robbing of orchards assistance I lent.

Those ways did increase as in age I grew old,
To plunder and rob I became the more bold,
Then in cursing and swearing no equal had I,
With lying and swearing and all that was bad.

To Barnet I went but my life was no better,
The tutor at length wrote my father a letter
Requesting he'd take me away for I should
Lead astray all the boys that at present were good.

My heart broken father to Barnet did come,
Resolving to take me once more to his home,
He heard of my deeds but knew not what to do,
Lest I should again such vile courses pursue.

He went o'er my ways like a father and friend,
And told me such ways in my ruin would end,
But alas to his council I turned a deaf ear,
And thought his behaviour to me was severe.

Then to Chelmsford as an apprentice I went,
I was bound to a pawnbroker by my own consent,
But wicked company once more led me astray,
And again returned to this dissolute way.

Till wagers and gambling took off all my store,
And then I resolved to rob for some more,
Two hundred and seventy pounds did I get,
But Satan did prompt me to greater sin yet.

My soul it was filled with the horrid desire
To set the whole house of my master on fire,
This deed I considered would set me secure,
So I went for to squander my ill gotten store.

Still justice pursued me and here I was brought,
To answer for this sad and terrible thought,
Tomorrow I'm doom'd to ascend the sad tree,
So I hope all will take a warning by me.

Tho' small may appear the crimes to begin,
To grow and to harden is the nature of sin,
O what my poor father and mother must feel,
To know in what manner my life I must yield.

After all their kind care and attention to me,
To come to this terrible end on the tree,
My heart is so hard that it will not relent,
Though often I strive I cannot repent.

Shepherd Printer   Broad Weir   Bristol
Travellers Supplied

A Warning to young Persons
The Life Trial and Confession of a boy aged 12 years at the
last Assizes at Chelmsford Essex

With horror we attempt to relate the progress of evil generally prevailing among children, through the corrupt example of their parents. Though we are constrained to confess that many a child through bad company wickedly followeth the dictates of their own will and often brings the hoary heads of honest parents with sorrow to the grave, yet while honest parents who discharge their duty stand justified in the sight of their maker, the horrors of a guilty conscience crieth to heaven for vengeance against such wretched parents as T King, a tradesman who after eloping from a popular country residence, concealed himself through deception and personated various characters, trades, etc., while committing notorious depredations throughout the kingdom. Then artfully obtained a settlement in East Smithfield, London, there he and his wife not only harboured the vilest of characters but wickedly encouraged their only son Tomas from an early period in life to practice lying, stealing etc. At length the parish humanely planned to bind him out as an apprentice at the age of seven years, but his wickedness prevented them from getting him a master, finally they bound him to a chimbley sweep who repented accepting him through plundering every place he was sent to work at, for which not only correction but imprisonment ensued. The honesty of his master (who often forced him to take back the property he had stolen) obtained a pardon for him twice, after setting fire to houses etc. Lastly his parents made him desert from his master and bound him to a gang of thieves who on the 10th April sent him down the chimney of Widow Penny a noted jeweller in London, where he unbolted the shop window shutter out of which his ringleader cut a pane of glass, while he with a dark lantern handed out the most valuable of articles he was detected though his leaders made their escape, for which he was capitally indicted tried and found guilty Death in the 12th year of his age to the astonishment of many. The boy confessed at last of several cruel murders and made a discovery of several noted robbers, now at liberty yet we hope not only to hear of their detection but that the wonderful life, trial, shocking confession and dreadful end of this youth with the awful state of

*34, who are now under sentence of death, together with 76 ordered for
transportation, may produce a lasting warning to the world at large.*

> *Ye mothers who have tender hearts
> I pray you lend an ear,
> Of a little boy at twelve years old
> A mournful tale you'll hear,
> Condemned of late of shocking crimes,
> Through his parents deeds, you see,
> You'd weep and cry to see him die,
> All on the gallows tree.*
>
> *When he was sentenced at the bar,
> The court was drowned in tears,
> To see a child so young cut off,
> And in his infant years,
> With piercing cries his mother mad
> And tearing hair she went,
> In Bedlam's chains she now remains,
> And his father to prison went*
>
> *The hardest heart would melt to tears,
> To hear this boy's sad moan,
> At the bar, he screamed and trembled,
> When his sentence was made known,
> Pick pockets at fairs, he then declared,
> His parents made him comply
> To join a cruel gang to murder and rob,
> For which he's doomed to die.*
>
> *All tender parents who have children dear
> Take warning by this book,
> May children's hearts be all renewed,
> While in it they do look,
> May they be brought to feel and see
> Their danger night and day,
> And pray the Lord to guide their steps,
> To shun bad company.*

Be warn'd, my little children dear,
By this poor boy's down fall,
Pray keep from bad company,
And God will bless you all.
O think how this poor little boy
Laments his woeful fate
On a gallows high now forced to die,
How dreadful is his case.

Each human heart now knows the past
That condemned this tender boy,
Wickedness and pride, that horrid guide,
By deceit hath him destoyed.
Religious thoughts he ne'er was taught,
Church or prayers he was never nigh,
Thro' improper care from parents dear,
This boy is condemned to die.

Bonner   Printer   adjoining St John's Gate Bristol

The first case of murder that can be dated to be issued on a ballad sheet was that of W Constable by Mary May. The whole ballad was quoted by Mayhew in *London Labour and the London Poor* as   a   fine example of this kind of literature; he says:

"I cannot refrain from calling the reader's attention to the 'copy of the verses' touching Mary May. I give them entire for they seem to me to contain all the elements which made the old ballads popular – the rushing at once into the subject – and the homely reflections, though crude to all educated persons, are, nevertheless, well adapted to enlist the sympathy and appreciation of the class of hearers to whom they are addressed."

The events surrounding the case were brought to light in the trail and fully described in *The Times* for 25th July, 1848.

Mary May, 28 years old (a replusive-looking woman) lived with her husband and children in the small village of Wix a few miles from Harwich, where she kept a grocers' or chandlers' shop. Her half brother, William Constable (in other accounts of the indictment known as William Watts), got his living by doing odd jobs in the village, he shared a room in the house with another man called Simpson and was known in the village as Spratty Watts.

Mary May had joined her half brother in the false name of William Constable, to a benefit or burial society at Harwich and had insured his life, falsely representing his age as 8, when he was, in fact, 50, an age that would have disentitled him to be a member, collecting between nine and ten pounds when he died.

On the 8th of June, when William had returned home from his work, one of the children was sent to get some porter into which Mary put some powder, afterwards heating the drink in a saucepan. William drank this and almost immediately complained of excessive stomach pains. In the following days he was visited by two doctors, finally dying on 11th June.

From the trial it appears that Mary May had told her neighbours of her plans to use the money when William died, to buy a horse and cart and to set up a higgler's business. This and other rumours alerted the authorities and the body was exhumed and the traces of poison were found. Mary May was found guilty and executed on 15th August, 1848.

The Life, Trial, Confession and Execution of Mary May
for the Murder of W Constable, her halfbrother, by Poison,
at Wix, near Manningtree.

[Then follows a short account of the last hours of Mary May before she was hung.]

Copy of Verses

The solemn bell for me doth toll,
And I am doom'd to die
(For murdering my brother dear,)
Upon a tree so high.
For gain I did premeditate
My brother for to slay –
Oh, think upon the dreadful fate
Of wretched Mary May

Chorus
Behold the fate of Mary May
Who did for gain her brother slay

In Essex boundary I did dwell,
My brother lived with me,
In a little village called Wix,
Not far from Manningtree,
In a burial club I entered him,
On purpose him to slay:
And to obtain the burial fees
I took his life away

One eve he to his home return'd,
Not thinking he was doom'd
To be sent by a sister's hand
Unto the silent tomb.
His tea for him I did prepare,
And in it poison placed,
To which I did administer,
How dreadful was his case.

Before he long the poison took,
In agony he cried,
Upon him I in scorn did look, –
At length my brother died.
Then to the grave I hurried him,
And got him out of sight,
But God ordain'd this cruel deed,
Should soon be brought to light.

I strove the money to obtain,
For which I did him slay,
For which, alas, suspicion fell,
On guilty Mary May.
The poison was discovered,
Which caused me to bewail,
And I my trial to await
Was sent to Chelmsford jail.

*And for this most atrocious deed
I at the bar was placed,
The jury found me guilty, -
How dreadful was my case
The judge the dreadful sentence pass'd
And solemn said to me,
You must return from whence you came,
And thence unto the tree.*

*On earth I can no longer dwell
There's nothing can me save,
Hark! I hear the mournful knell,
Which calls me to the grave.
Death appears in ghostly forms
To summon me below;
See, the fatal bolt is drawn,
And Mary May must go.*

*Good people all, of each degree,
Before it is too late,
See me on the fatal tree,
And pity my sad fate,
My guilty heart stung with grief,
With agony and pain -
My tender brother I did slay
That fatal day for gain.*

In October, 1850, another murder was committed that caused great interest and long reports in *The Times.**

Jael Denny was 21 and lived with her mother and stepfather at Doddinghurst, not far from Chelmsford. They had moved into a cottage after having lived in with a Mr Drory as housekeeper and labourer on his off-hand farm that he looked after for his father. Like many other country girls she had been in service at various situations before returning to her parents' cottage. From the trial it appears that Mr Drory and Jael Denny had been courting for some time and that Jael was pregnant, expecting his child in two or three months' time. Drory though was thinking of marrying a Miss Gibbings, and even went so far as to get Jael

***The Times** 4 April, 5 April, 8 March, 10 March, 1851.

to write a note, to say that the baby was not his. Then, on 12th October, 1850, between 6 and 7 o'clock, Jael hurried out of the cottage, leaving her tea half-eaten, to keep an appointment with Drory. She was found by her stepfather next morning in a nearby field, strangled. Drory was found guilty and sentenced to hang in March, 1851.

So far I have found four ballads about this murder. Copy of verses on Drory and Jael Denny by E Hodges, from Pitts Wholesale Toy Warehouse, 81 Dudley Street, Seven Dials: Confessions of Thos Drory, and The Lamentation of Thos Drory who now lays in Chelmsford Jail for the murder of Jael Denny, by Disley Printer, 16 Arthur Street, St Giles: and, lastly, Trial and Confession of Thos Drory for the murder of Jael Denny, printed at 2 & 3 Monmouth Court by J Catnach.

Trial and Confession of Thos Drory
for the murder of Jael Denny
Verses
Tune   The wealthy farmer's son

Come all false hearted young men
And listen to my song,
'Tis of a cruel murder
That lately has been done,
On the body of a maiden fair,
The truth I will unfold,
The bare relation of the deed
Will make your blood run cold.

Near Brentwood town in Essex,
Jael Denny she did dwell,
And with her parents did reside,
Till this to her befell.
Her cheeks were like the blushing rose,
All in the month of May,
Which made this wicked young man
This unto her to say

"Jael Denny, my charming creature,
You have my heart ensnared,
My love is such I am resolved
To wed you I declare."
Thus by his false, deluding tongue,
Poor Jael she was beguilded
And soon to her misfortune
By him she proved with child.

One fatal day at evening,
This young man did repair
To a lonely place across the fields
To meet poor Jael there.
Saying, "Come, my dear, we'll take a walk
Across yon flowery field,
And then the secrets of my heart,
To you I will reveal."

Horrible and Bar-bari-ous Murder ot Poor
JAEL DENNY,
THE ILL-FATED VICTIM OF THOMAS DRORY.

O then this wicked young man,
A rope he did provide,
And all unknown to his true love,
Concealed it by his side,
When to the fatal spot they came,
These words to her did say,
"All on this night I will
Your precious life betray."

O then this wicked young man said,
"No mercy I will show."
He took the rope all from his side,
Which round her neck he threw,
But she still smiling, said to him,
While trembling with fear,
"Ah Thomas, Thomas, spare my life,
Think on your baby dear."

Twice more then this horrid rope,
Around her neck he drew,
Her throat was torn and mangled,
Most dreadful for to view,
Her hands and arms and beautous face,
He bit and bruised, we see,
While he did kneel upon her breast,
What must her feeling be.

O then this villain taken was,
And cast for death, we hear,
And soon before the Judge of all,
He trembling must appear,
Then oh beware of flattering tongues,
For they'll your ruin prove,
So may you crown your future days
In comfort peace and love.

Printed at 2 and 3 Monmouth Court
Bloomsbury

The Lamentation of Thos Drory
Who now lies in Chelmsford Jail, for the Murder of
Jael Denny, his sweetheart

You passers by one moment stay,
And ponder on what I now do say,
And when my sad history I've told through,
That how false pride has caused me to rue

For murder I alas bewail,
My wretched fate in Chelmsford Jail.

Thomas Drory it is my name,
And till this time have been free from shame,
Oh cruel fate, with murder rife,
That I should take my true love's life.

In affluence I was bred and born,
With property to live upon,
At Great Burstead my homestead stood,
When evil deeds o'er shadowed good.

My first affections they were placed,
On poor Jael Denny, ah sad disgrace,
Who should have been my lawful wife,
If I had not been tempted to take her life.

I loved her long, I loved her true,
The truth I now will tell to you,
Until her virtue I did beguile,
And my true love she proved with child.

It was then my love it turned to hate,
Which ended in her dreadful fate,
I courted another in Brentwood Town,
Which caused me to inflict double wound.

The tempting fiend it appeared to me,
"Your love, Miss Denny, stands in your way
You must not take her for your wife."
I determined to take her life.

With false promises I persuaded her,
Near Doddinghurst to meet me there,
"Do come, my dear," I to her did say,
"And we will fix our wedding day."

She to her mother hastened home,
And the good tidings to her did own,
Saying, "Oh, Drory met me this very night,
And he has swore to make me his wife."

At the appointed time she met me there,
Saying, "Thomas, I am glad you're here."
Poor innocent she little dreamt
That to murder her was my intent.

We walked along, nor once did stop,
Till we reached a lonely spot,
Where with my murderous hand a rope,
I passed around my victim's throat.

For mercy she aloud did call,
But no mercy to her did I show at all.
With blood my hands they are defiled,
I slew her and her unborn child.

Now it was discovered, as has been told,
The thoughts of it makes my blood run cold,
My destiny I must await,
And justly meet my wretched fate.

You lovers all where'er you be,
A warning take, I pray by me,
Strive to walk in virtuous ways,
And happy may you pass your days.

Disley, Printer, 16, Arthur Street, High Street,
Saint Giles

Mayhew's informant also worked these particular sheets, although he did not seem to make very much money from their sale (He still made enough to buy a waistcoat and shirt).

"Then there was the 'Horrid and Inhuman Murder, committed by T Drory, on the body of Jael Denny at Doddinghurst, a village in Essex'. We worked it in every way. Drory had every chance given to him. We had half sheets, and copies of verses, and books. A very tidy book it was, setting off with showing how 'The secluded village of Doddinghurst has been the scene of a most determined and diabolical murder, the discovery of which early on Sunday the 12th, in the morning has thrown this part of the country into a painful state of excitement'. Well sir, well – very well; that bit was taken from a newspaper. Oh, we're not above acknowledging when we condescends to borrow from any of 'em. If you remember, when I saw you about the time, I told you I thought Jael Denny would turn out as good as Maria Martin. And without any joke or nonsense, sir, it really is a most shocking thing. But she didn't. The weather coopered her, poor lass! There was money in sight, and we couldn't touch it; it seemed washed away from us,* for you may remember how wet it was. I made a little by her, though, for all that I haven't done with Master Drory yet. If God spares my life, he shall make it up to me. Why now, sir, is it reasonable, that a poor man like me should take so much pains to make Drory's name known all over the country, and walk miles and miles in the rain to do it, and only get a few bob for my labours? It can't be thought on. When the Vile and Inhuman Seducer takes his trial, he must pay up my just claims. I'm not going to take all that trouble on his account, and let him off so easy."

*This comment clearly indicates how the ballad seller relied on good weather to sell ballads, as rain, etc., would damage the sheets as they were held on show in the sellers' hands. In bad weather the sale of ballads would be confined to dry places – the public house, farm kitchen, etc. This would, of course, restrict sales considerably.

Life and Times of James Catnach Charles Hindley.

There were so many different types of broadsides that hawkers often specialised in a particular
line. Tragedy Bill was a specialist in the sale of
murders, lamentations and last dying confessions. He
was probably not the only one and his type of patter
would have been widely used by other hawkers:

"Now, my kind friends and relations, here you
have, just printed and published, a full, true, and
pertickler account of the life, trial, character, confession, behaviour, condemnation, and hexecution of
that unfortunate malefactor, Richard Wilbyforce, who
was hexecuted on Monday last, 'for the small charge
of one ha'penny', and for the most horrible, dreadful
and wicked murder of Samuel - I mean Sarah
Spriggens, a lady's maid, young, tender, and handsome.
You have here every pertickler, of that which he did,
and that which he didn't. It's the most foul and
horrible murder that ever graced the annals of British
history? Here, my customers, you may read his
hexecution on the fatal scaffold. You may also read
how he met his victim in a dark and lonesome wood,
and what he did to her - 'For the small charge of a
ha'penny!' and further, you may read how he brought
her to London after that comes the murder, which is
worth all the money. And you read how the ghost
appeared to him and then to her parents. Then comes
the capture of the villain; also the trial, sentence, and
hexecution, showing how the ghost was in the act of
pulling his leg on one side, and the 'old gentleman' a
pulling on the other, waiting for his victim (my good
friends, fellow countrymen, and female women, excuse
my tears). But has Shakespeare says, 'Murder most
foul and unnatural', but you'll find this more foul and
unnatural than that or t'other - 'For the small charge
of a ha'penny!' Yus, my customers, to which is added
a copy of serene and beautiful verses, pious and
immoral, as wot he wrote with his own blood and a
skewer the night after - I mean the night before his
hexecution, addressed to you men and women of all
sexes - I beg pardon, but I mean classes (my friends
it's nothing to laugh at), for I can tell you the verses
is made three of the hardest-heartedest things cry as
never was - to wit, that is to say, namely - a over-

seer, a broker, and a policeman. Yes, my friends, I sold twenty-thousand copies of them this here morning, and could a' sold twenty thousand more than that if I could of but kept from crying – 'only a ha'penny!'"

Another murder that had as many ballad sheets as the previous took place in December, 1874, at Purfleet and in Grays Thurrock Museum a complete set of ballad sheets can be seen.

Alice Boughen was aged 5; she attended the Military Infant School in the Garrison at Purfleet. The young army schoolmaster, 21-year-old Richard Coutts, who was also a gunner with the 15th Battery of Artillery, murdered her. Unable to deposit the body in the river, he hid it near a boat shed, where it was later found. Coutts was found guilty and hung.*

Four ballad sheets have been discovered by Terry Carney, who subsequently reprinted them in *Panorama* Nos. 20 & 23, the journal of the Thurrock Local History Society.

THE
OUTRAGE & MURDER
On a Little Child at Purfleet
A little girl named Alice Boughen, was supposed to have been dreadfully outraged and murdered by a School-master, on Wednesday: she left her home at 2 o'clock, to go to school. At half-past 3 she left the room to go into the back, and was not seen alive afterward.
Tune   Just before the battle mother

You parents dear that love your children,
*   Just listen to this dreadful deed,*
A little girl she has been murdered,
*   It will cause each mother's heart to bleed;*
Poor child she was outraged by a soldier,
*   Then brutally murdered as we're told,*
At Purfleet poor Alice Boughen,
*   She was just 5 Years and ten months old*

***The Essex Independent and Farmers' Gazette** Monday, 8th March, 1875.

Lamentation of R. Coates,

Who now lies under Sentence of Death, for the wilful murder of Alice Boughen, the daughter of a soldier in the Royal Artillery at Purfleet.

At Chelmsford, on Friday. March 5th, before the Lord Chief Justice, Richard Coates, 21 years of age, a gunner in the Royal Artillery, was charged with the wilful murder of Alice Boughen.   The prisoner pleaded Not Guilty.

Alice Boughen, aged five years and ten months, and her brother James, who was younger, children of James Boughen, servant to Captain Wood   On the 9th of December, in the afternoon the children went to school, a little before 3 the girl left the room to go into the back yard,   Soon after she was followed by the schoolmaster, who did not return to the school until half-past 3, when he dismissed his pupils, and gave Alice's bonnet and jacket to her brother, telling him that his sister had gone out and could not be found   A strict search was then made, and about half-past 6 the next morning the body was discovered under some wet grass, dead, her legs and other parts being covered with blood,

After an immense mass of evidence, among which it was proved as to finding blood on the prisoner's shirt and trousers, a spot of blood was also found by prisoner's bed, and there were marks of blood on the window sill close to the bed.   The Jury returned a verdict of Guilty, and the Judge passed Sentence of Death.   The trial lasted 3 days.

O listen to the said Lamentatation
  Of Richard Coates who soon will be
In Springfield gaol as I will mention,
  Deprived of life on the gallows tree.
My victim's blood it cries for vengeance,
  To still my conscience in vain I try
O let me now in sincere repentance,
  Confess ere I upon the scaffold die.

Poor Alice Broughten, thy fate was dreadful,
  On the scaffold see your murderer go,
Your little soul it rests in heaven;
  While Richard Coates seeks the shades below.

By counsel now I've been assisted,
  To save my life in vain they tried,
But now alas I've been convicted,
  I would I'd in my cradle died.
I might have lived and been respected,
  In battle perhaps met death so brave,
But in a gloomy cell dejected,
  I now must fill a murderer's grave.

The jury they have found me guilty,
  I vainly sought my crime to hide,
Poor little Alice now gazing on me,
  Her form is always by my side.
O, cursed be that fatal morning,
  When you on me did so confide.

For parents now would not be mourning.
  And Alice dear would not have died.

The time it now is fast approaching,
  When I must leave this world of woe,
And for this deed on Alice Broughen,
  Unto my fearful death I go.
Her little hands now point towards me,
  Her form now in my cell I see.
She's always present, she never leaves me,
  Until I die on the gallows tree.

Can such a villian ask for mercy
  As here condemned in my cell I lie,
My aged father is weeping for me,
  And brokenhearted mother cries
From God above. let me ask for mercy,
  That little creature denied below,
Her dreadful death I'm now repenting,
  Ere I upon the scaffold go

So all young men pray take a warning.
  By Richard Coates—his dreadful fate,
Behold me on that fatal morning,
  Repenting when it is too late.
I hear the hangman now approaching,
  The solemn bell for me does toll,
For murdering poor Alice Broughton,
  May God have mercy on my soul.

Chorus:
Poor little child her death was so dreadful,
How sad her fate to die so young,
Outraged and murdered by a soldier,
At Purfleet this deed was done.

Poor Alice dear sweet little angel,
  Was carried by this monster bold,
Into a field for his vile purpose,
  Then she was murdered as we're told;
To hide her quite the cursed monster,
  He concealed his victim in some hay,
Near the Magazine her frozen body,
  Was found a mass of lifeless clay,

Then he sent home her little brother,
  With his sister's hat and jacket too,
The father he was broken hearted,
  At first he scarce knew what to do;
No doubt dear Alice cried for mercy,
  He heeded not her pityous cry,
On this little dear he had no pity,
  Poor child a dreadful death to die.

Oh, what must be the parents feelings,
  Now their dear daughter is no more,
When she was found the site was dreadful
  Poor child lay weltring in her gore,
May her soul rest with its maker,
  Where angels dwell both night and day,
At her tender age she had no notion,
  That fiend would take her life away.

Richard Coote, was a school master,
  Of the Royal Artillery as we hear,
His little victim suffered dreadful,
  Her nose was torn away we hear;
The murderer then to stop her screaming,
  He prest his hand on her sweet face,
With her little strength she struggled with him,
  On his clothes her innocent blood was traced.

In 1894 at Chelmsford Assizes, James Canham Read was tried for the murder of Florence Dennis.

James Read lived with his wife and 8 children at 57 Jamaica Street, Stepney, near the Royal Albert Dock where he was employed as a clerk. In August, 1882, he became friendly with Mrs Ayriss, with whom he had an affair. Mrs Ayriss was the elder sister of Florence Dennis and she introduced them. Read, under an assumed name, began to correspond with Florence while she was living with her younger sister in High Street, Sheerness. Eventually Florence became pregnant by Read and it was at this time, having started yet another affair with a Miss Kempton, that Read's private life began to get complex. He met Florence Dennis at Prittlewell while she was on a visit to West Street, Leigh. Here on a footpah with a hedge on one side and high corn growing on the field side, he shot Florence and threw her body in the ditch, where it was later discovered. Taking an amount from the Dock Company office, Read fled to a cottage owned by Miss Kempton at Mitcham. Here he allowed his beard to grow and bought a new suit in Croydon to complete his disguise - being shortly after arrested and charged. He was found guilty and hung at Springfield Prison, Chelmsford, in December, 1894.

The whole story of this crime may have disappeared into oblivion, finding its resting place in the newspaper files of the past. Strangely, two broadside ballads came to light, mixed in with a collection of Dutch broadsides in a folio in the British Library.

Southend Crime
Florrie Dennis found shot
Capture of Read at Mitcham
[woodcut of Read, Dennis and 3 children]
J C Read the mystery   The man of many wives
Descriptive Songs on the Southend Murder
Tune   Teddy O'Neale

In a pretty town close to the ocean,
In Essex well known as Southend on Sea,
A murder has thrown the town in commotion,
As brutal a murder as ever could be.

The victim, we're told, has been a young lady,
Who had been deceived by her lover, they say,
Shot through the head and thrown in the water,
Poor Florence Dennis to death led astray.

Chorus:
At Southend on Sea this crime was committed,
Poor Florence Dennis in life led astray,
Her murderer, we hope, will not be permitted
To take her dear life in this inhuman way.

A man, we are told, is charged on suspicion,
If he's not guilty he'll have to explain,
For some little time he's been lodging at Mitcham,
With a female and baby in a different name.
He has told many stories his history giving,
A tale of deception if it proves true,
They say, he's a wife and family living,
But yet keeping company with these other two.

The poor girl he lived with struck down with terror,
She seem'd in a moment o'er loaded with shame,
The man she had loved to be charged with murder,
To her he had given a quite different name.
To the scene of the murder detectives convey'd him,
Thousands had gathered his arrival by train,
If they had their way they would lynch him,
But until he's proved guilty quite safe he'll remain.

He says he can prove that he is not guilty,
Why don't he do so and then be set free,
That he should disguise himself seems a pity,
Innocent people don't do so, you see.
Within a short time he has been wearing glasses,
Which alters a man's appearance, we know,
He'll have a good chance as the time passes,
His reason for doing this he'll have to show.

Three women, we see, by someone or other
Are cruelly treated and lost to the world,
Respectable people with fathers and mothers,
Who in disguise are in misery hurl'd.

But altho' we have known the innocent suffer,
In these days we exercise every care,
The evidence given by one and the other
No judge or jury to alter must dare.

Karl Kohl had lived in England for some time and in September, 1864, he went back to visit Germany. Returning in October, he married and moved into a house in Hoy Street, Plaistow, where he let some rooms to lodgers. On the ship during his return journey he met Christian Furhop and they became very friendly, as Furhop could not speak English and was a stranger to England. Furhop at first stayed with Mrs Warren at 3 Nelson Street, Plaistow Marshes, trusting her with his money, watch and rings. He afterwards moved his lodging to Kohl's house in Hoy Street.

On the 3rd of November, 1864, they walked together along the side of the Thames, where Furhop was last seen alive. Kohl, although found guilty, never admitted to the murder of his friend, no blood being found on his clothing although the body was badly mutilated. He was executed in January, 1865, at Chelmsford.*

Dreadful Murder
at Plaistow

On Wednesday, Nov 2nd a human body was discovered in the reed beds Plaistow Marshes. The head was found buried in the ground about 12 yards from the body. Rats had devoured the hands and the body was shocklingly mutilated. A German, named Kohl, recognised the remains to be his particular friend, who had lodged with him and his wife. He said that the murdered man's name was Furhop, a native of Holland, and that they had both sailed from Hamburgh to London as fellow passengers. From information received, Kohl was taken into custody, and from the over whelming evidence produced he was fully committed for trial. The hatchet supposed to be used by the prisoner in slaying Furhop, has been found.

*The Times 13th, 27th, 28th January, 1865.

Franz Muller's fate we're all aware,
Is past and far gone o'er,
The fourteenth of November,
Eighteen hundred and sixty four.
Another dreaful deed's been done,
By his countryman, we see,
It will make your blood run cold to hear
The Essex tragedy.

The German Kohl, a murderer base,
Such deeds will. never end,
In Essex in the Plaistow-marsh,
Kohl killed his bosom friend.

We recollect John Thurtell,
That was in past gone years,
When Thurtell, Hunt and Probert
Did murder William Ware,
Who close by Gill's Hill Cottage,
In a pond murdered was found
And we recollect James Greenacre,
Who murdered Hannah Brown.

And this dreadful atrocious German,
Mark well what I relate,
Had a young friend, a countryman,
How dreadful was his fate,
To lead him for a lonely walk,
The villain did engage,
Poor unsuspecting young man,
Three and twenty years of age.

Kohl took him to the Marshes,
Where he led him astray,
He was armed with a hatchet,
Determined him to slay.
Before him passed the waving reeds,
For a few paltry pounds,
As behind his bosom friend he walked,
He felled him to the ground.

His crimson blood in streams did flow
And stained the fatal ground,
He killed and robbed his bosom friend,
For a few paltry pounds.
His head from off his body,
He cut, as we may see,
And then he had completed
The Essex tragedy.

The body of his bosom friend
Was headless when they found,
And his head the villain buried
Seven inches 'neath the ground
He was going to sail for Germany,
Justice he could not pass,
But like the culprit Muller,
Was the villain caught at last.

He now awaits his trial,
In a dungeon is in gloom,
And fast approaching is the time,
The rogue will know his doom.
Evidence is clear against him,
There's no doubt he did the deed,
And to the bar of Justice
He will be placed with speed.

Of all the cruel murders,
The world of late did see,
There's not been one more dreadful
Than this Essex tragedy.
No sooner had one German
Met his untimely end,
But we have see one of his countrymen,
Has killed a bosom friend.

Disley, Printer, 57, High Street, St Giles.

In 1851 there was a theft of money from the Royal Ordnance Powder Works at Waltham Abbey, the money consisting of the wage roll and twelve pounds belonging to the deputy storekeeper, amounting to £500 in all.

Four men were tried for the robbery. G Rowe, described as a tall, respectable-looking man whose occupation was innkeeper of the Three Compasses in Stewardstone Street (now just called The Compasses): J Cornish and C Eves were in the service of the Ordnance factory as mill men and, during Sundays and holidays, as watchmen: the fourth was Jesse Griffiths, described as an itinerant fishdealer.

It appeared that Eves' brother was accused of being mixed up in the robbery. Rowe had given him a bottle of brandy to keep him quiet, but finding that the Government had offered a reward of £50, he told all he knew to the Ordnance officials. As a result, the four men were arrested.

We are Lucky Chaps at Waltham

We are to Waltham home returned,
A set of chaps who are not shabby
We did expect to get blowed up,
From Chelmsford coming to Waltham Abbey.

Hard was our lot - powder and shot -
When we got in a dreadful row sir,
So gay and funny about some money,
We are liberated - beef and powder.

Three of us are home returned,
Although the gentlemen were shabby,
In Chelmsford we acquitted was
And toddled home to Waltham Abbey.

But our friend who dealt in beer,
Sorry indeed we are he nicked it,
It made us all feel very queer,
When the Essex jury him convicted

THE POWDER MILLS, WALTHAM.

Ten years we sorry are to say,
Him to whose house we oft resorted,
Is doomed to go to Botany Bay,
Thro' powder he has got transported.

May heaven soothe his aching mind,
And be his family protecting,
To any usage that's unkind,
We hope they never will subject him.

And we shall ever cautious be,
And keep away from harm and row, sir,
And never to our dying day,
Will we meddle with the nasty powder.

Chelmsford is a curious place,
Inside their walls they use folks shabby,
We hope to never go again,
One inch away from Waltham Abbey.

Joyfully we left the bar,
And nimbly pushed through the crowd, sir,
May the d------ break our rhubarb sticks,
If ever again we touch the powder.

The last ballad in this chapter comes from the notebook of William James Coakham, who lived sometime in Walthamstow and was compiled, according to the title page, in the 1860s.*

I cannot be absolutely sure that the verses are from a broadside ballad sheet, but it has the ring and metre of a ballad composition.

In 1790 the House of Correction built in 1609 in East Street, Barking, was examined and found that the wards were too small, with offensive sewers running through them and no sick or work rooms. The yard was insecure and prisoners were denied access. In 1791/2 a new house to serve a wider area was erected in North Street, Barking. It stood on $\frac{1}{2}$ acre of ground surrounded by garden, keeper's house, separate yards,

* Extracts subsequently reprinted in **Across the Years**, Walthamstow memories.

work rooms for men and women, and an infirmary. The men were employed in picking oakum. By 1806 there were 14 prisoners. In the early 1830s the Quarter Sessions decided to build a new house at Little Ilford. The old Barking house was then sold in 1834 and soon demolished.

In 1860 the jail was reorganised for prisoners on remand or serving short sentences. It was finally closed in 1878 and demolished soon after. The site, now partly covered by houses and shops, was on the north side of Romford Road between Worcester and Gloucester Roads.*

Ilford Jail

Good people all give answer, I pray, and listen well to what I say,
To my misfortunes, great and small, if you listen now I'll tell you all
I once did live a joyous life, devoid of care, devoid of strife,
I could go to bed and fall asleep, no ugly sprites would round me creep
But Oh! the touts and Cupids, gad, they nearly sent me raving mad,
So they clapt me into the King's Royal Mail, and sent me off to
Ilford Jail.

So right about face, turn out your toes, chuck a good chest and away you goes,
That's to the place to make you quail. Oh! jolly good luck to Ilford

Now when we got to the end of the rout, the turnkey turned my pockets out,
To see if I had got such stuff as blunt, or grub, tobacco or snuff,
They took me then to try my size, colour of my hair, colour of my eyes,
Length of my nose from root tip, whether I'd hair on my top lip,
Straight with me to a yard they goes, there they made me change my clothes
All came out and did me hail, 'Here's another new lad for Ilford Jail."

***Victoria County History of Essex Vol. 6.**

I trotted and walked about in the yard, thinking my case was very hard,

When all at once I heard a din 'twas the deputy warder 'Fall in.'

Then bawling down the yard did go, like brutes turned out in a wild beast show,

Some crackt in skin, and some in mind, and some through cracks showed their behinds,

Then one by one went round a tub and got the County allowance of grub,

Blowed our kites out like a sail, skilly and whack in Ilford Jail.

When half past four came, one of 'em said, he thought it time to go to bed,

And truth I long'd from them to creep, because I wanted to get some sleep,

When the turnkey shouts as stiff as starch, 'Right about face and then Quick March.'

We did and caused a curious crush, like monkeys walking round a bush,

Such a rattling of clogs, clinking of keys, quaking of bellies, and shaking of knees,

And cussing of beds as hard as a nail oh! 'twould kill the devil in Ilford Jail.

At five the next morning, up we got, each stoned his cell and got quite hot,

And then about the yard did lurch, until 'twas time to go to church,

And there such dresses met my view, one leg was yellow, another was blue,

One cap was black, another was green, such comical clothes sure I'd never seen,

One arm was red, another was grey, in came the parson to preach and pray.

He told us Elijah went up in a cloud, Lazarus walked about in a shroud

Jonah lived inside a whale, he was better off there than in Ilford Jail.

BALLADS PRINTED IN ESSEX

We have now looked at the various types of ballads that were printed in London by the big Victorian presses of Catnach, Such and their contemporaries. So far only the contents of the ballads described have originated in Essex, the events having found their way to London either by oral transmission or copied from the early newspapers, these events being turned into rhyme and circulated as ballads on broadsheets. We can now see from these a cross-section of ballad types and have a fairly clear idea of what news, events, etc., would be suitable for issue on a broadside ballad.

Printing in Essex has never been an important industry, and information on printers in the county is very scarce. Nearly all of the printing houses in the county were small family affairs. Even those that produced the various county newspapers did not aspire to large businesses. A typical Essex printer is described in his advertisment as:

"R W Cullingford, General printer, Publisher, Bookseller, and Stationer 153 High Street, Colchester. A house well known and widely patronised in the printing and stationery trade is that of Mr R W Cullingford, whose career during the six years of his proprietorship has been one of gratifying success. The premises are admirably situated at 153 High Street. The shop is well appointed, and stocked with a capital selection of books and stationery. General printing is an important feature of Mr Cullingford's business, and the printing-rooms are replete with the most improved machinery and the newest type and appliances. Attention must be directed to another branch, namely, the circulating library, which is well patronised and highly appreciated by the reading public of Colchester. The productions of this house will bear comparison for excellence and moderate charges with an similar concern in the district. The proprietor's practical experience and well-directed energy have secured for this enterprise an eminent position in the town. No effort has been spared to attain this object, and Mr Cullingford is the recipient of the well-deserved esteem of a large cliency."*

The printing press had remained more or less the same from the days of Caxton to the late 18th century. The first real improvements came when the handle, bar and screw were replaced by a system of levers, and at the same time, iron began to replace the wooden parts of the old presses. The Stanhope, Columbian and Albion presses were built along these lines, but were still only capable of printing single sheets, at about 250 per hour. These would have been the types of press that Essex printing houses were most probably equipped with.

Broadside ballads were produced locally, although on a much reduced scale. Evidence from sheets that have survived show that these were most probably of a one-off order for some local customer or a special event. Even so, some presses did a good trade in ballad sheets.

The earliest surviving sheet that I have found came from the press of William Keymer of Colchester, where it is believed the earliest printing press in Essex was situated.

William Keymer was born in 1731 and is believed to be the son of Robert Keymer of Colchester. In 1760 at the age of 28 he married Ann Edwards (30) of St Runwald's Parish. Robert and William were advertising the sale of books as early as 1750 at the Moot Hall in Colchester, printing and publishing at the Bible and Star near the White Hart Inn in St Peter's Parish until 1813. Robert also had a branch shop in Hadleigh in Suffolk that was advertised in the *Ipswich Journal* as early as 1750, continuing

***Industries of the Eastern Counties Business Review, 1888 – 1890.**

until 1762. In 1765 William moved to St Runwald's Parish to premises said to have belonged to the Keymer family for one hundred years. He died on 29th May, 1813, aged 82, his business being taken over by W Keymer, Junior, on whose retirement in 1821 it passed into other hands.
William Keymer combined his bookselling with that of chemist. Interestingly enough, many of these 18th century printers carried on this combined business. Another Colchester printer, John Pillborough, whose shop in 1736 was 'over against St Nicholas Church', where he performed 'all manner of printing works, publishing the Essex Mercury or Colchester weekly Journal, supplying blank Warrants, and receipts, bound books and sold elixirs, cordials etc. in bottles', suggests that he was in the chemist trade too. In *Essex at Work* by F J Brown an Essex bookshop is quoted as:

> *"There pamphlets, lists of cures in printed bills,*
> *Phails and wafers, gallipots and quills,*
> *And wooden cuts that country maids entice,*
> *And ballads, headed by some gay device,*
> *The gaudy knave of clubs and colour'd chart,*
> *And piles of shining wax, dispos'd with art,*
> *Adorn the jutting sash, contriv'd for show."*

The combination of these two trades was practised by John Cluer in the 1720s. His press was at the Maiden Head, at the lower end of Bow Church Yard in Cheapside, London. Being one of the leading publishers of chapbooks and broadsides of that period, he also sold patent medicines and specifics, Daffey's Elixir Salutis, Hungary Water, Dr Bateman's Pectoral Drops and the True Antidote against Bugs.

King Coel
A song
in honour of the
Loyal Colchester Volunteers
Sung at the theatre, Colchester
on Tuesday Nov 14 1797
Second edition
Tune   The Roast Beef of Old England

King Coel of old, of great martial renown,*
With his brave Volunteers protected our town,
As in history's page with truth handed down.
*   O the great sons of King Coel,*
His loyal and brave Volunteers.

Invaded, they triumph'd on Victory's wing,
What conquests, what glory, from Union spring!
No democrats then – they were all for their king
*   O the great sons, etc.*

Love's Volunteer Helena† ended this strife,
Took Constantius captive – nay bound him for life,
And at once made a permanent peace – and a wife,
*   O the fair daughter of Coel,*
A loyal and true Volunteer.

They were Volunteer archers, as history goes,
No trifles (like moderns) with quire and bows,
The prize was no bauble – the conquest of foes.
*   O the great sons, etc.*

'Gainst Cromwell, that regicide matchless in guile,
See your own Volunteers the last troops of this isle,
Stand a siege to the last, with brave Lucas and Lisle.
*   O the great sons, etc.*

Thus from Romans to Saxons, from Saxons to Danes,
From conquering Normans to all future reigns,
Volunteers have adorn'd and protected these plains.
*   O the great sons, etc.*

'Tis ours to be arm'd against perils to come
Froma siege or a mob – we've no business to roam –
Foreign foes we'll repel – and look sometimes at home!
         O the great sons, etc.

But this bugbear Invasion – th'alarm of the day,
An attempt that must end in skirmishing fray,
Howe, Vincent, and Dundas, has quite done away½
           O the great sons, etc.

Should the war, God forbid it, the worst events bring,
We'd die sword in hand – no inglorious thing,
In defence of our Laws, Constition, and King,
O the great sons of King Coel
         His loyal and brave Volunteers.

** Coel II King of Colchester – Morant, B.1, p.28.*
† Helena, the daughter of King Coel, married Constantinus the Roman
general, and in consequence of the nupitals a peace was concluded –
Morant, B.1, p.27.
   The profits, if any, arising from the sale of this song will be
      given by the Publisher toward the relief of a Distressed
                  Family in Colchester.
   Colchester, printed and sold by W Keymer, jun.

We have very little information about the next Colchester printer, Isaac Marsden, but it appears he was probably the son of John Marsden, a framework stocking knitter from Mansfield, Nottinghamshire, who settled in Colchester around 1776. He married Hannah Jarrolds in 1796 and, in July, 1800, applied for a licence to print in his private house in St Nicholas Parish. This was required under the Act to suppress societies who spread seditions and treasonable practices:

"To the Clerk of the peace for the county of Essex or his deputy.

"I, Isaac Marsden, of Colchester in the said count of Essex, Printer, do hereby declare that I have a printing press and types for printing which I propose to use for printing within my dwelling house, within the parish of Saint Nicholas in the Borough of Colchester afore said and which I require to be certified for the purpose in pursuance of an act paper in the 39th year of the Reign of his Majesty King George the third entitled an act for the more effectual suppression of societies established for seditions and treasonable purpose there after preventing treasonable and seditious practices. Witnessed my hand this 23rd day of July 1800 signed in the presence of John Mason. I Marsden."

Sometime between 1800 and 1813 he formed a partnership with one Oliver, as in April, 1813, a brick dwelling house (built the previous year) in East Stockwell Street was up for sale, due to the partnership being dissolved. Isaac Marsden then returned to his former shop at 56, High Street. In 1814 he was indicted for publishing a libel on William Smith, a GP, and in 1815 was in the Castle gaol for printing it. He printed various chapbooks for sale by himself in Colchester and for London booksellers. Another publishing line and one that is of interest to us was his involvement with printing ballad sheets.

The four still in existence were printed for S Carpue of London. Whether they were commissioned by him for sale in his shop, or if he acted as sales outlet for Isaac Marsden, is unknown.

Leslie Shepherd, in his book *John Pitts ballad printer of Seven Dials London*, gives an address of a Daniel Henry Carpue of 177 Great Saffron Hill, who applied for a printing certificate in 1831 under the same Act as Isaac Marsden. There may have been some relation between these two (S Carpue and D Carpue, father and son?).

The ballads on three of the surviving sheets are all popular songs from the theatres and pleasure gardens of the late 18th and early 19th centuries and are of little interest to the present book, but the fourth is a most fascinating account of a balloon journey across Essex and deserves a full explanation.

The full title of this sheet is: Garnerin's Balloon, Sung by Mr Johnnot at Astleys Amphimheatre.*

Andre Jacques Garnerin was born in 1767 and made his first balloon ascent at the age of 19, subsequently making ascents from various cities in Europe. His other claim to fame was to be the first man to make a successful parachute jump, once performing this feat over London on 21 September, 1802.

Phillip Astley was born in 1742, son of a cabinetmaker in Newcastle-under-Lyme. By 17 he was an expert horseman, running away from home, he enlisted in Colonel Eliott's new regiment, the 15th Dragoons as a horsebreaker and roughrider. He was discharged from the army at 24 and continued to practice horsebreaking in Islington.

Where Waterloo Station and a maze of streets darken the earth between Westminster Bridge Road and Blackfriars Road, there lay, in the 1760s, a broad ditch surrounded by fields and market gardens. A path way led through the fields and for its use pedestrians paid a halfpenny toll - hence its name, Halfpenny Hatch. It was in one of the fields adjoining Halfpenny Hatch that Phillip Astley in 1768 gave the first circus performance in the world. His performances grew grander as time passed and, in 1779, Astley roofed over the whole of his establishment and advertised it as The Amphitheatre Riding House, Westminster Bridge, the most complete building of its kind in Europe. Not only did Phillip Astley perform riding tricks in the ring, but from the early days he had displays of tumbling, rope dancing, swordsmanship. More and more musical entertainments were added until in 1788 it was almost half the bill. Always seeking for further attractions, in 1784 Astley hit upon another method of self-advertisment, by sending up a balloon from St George's Fields.

The Amphitheatre was burnt down twice, the second time in 1803, and was rebuilt each time bigger than the last. Phillip Astley died in 1813, the Amphitheatre being taken over by the Sanger circus family in 1871 and eventually pulled down in 1893.*
*The Greatest Show on Earth M Wilson Disher.

So this ballad includes at least two 'firsts' and is of historical interest, as well as being locally printed.

Garnerin's Balloon
Sung by Mr Johnnot
at
Astley Amphimheatre

O Brawl no more gossips, of things out of tune,
For the wonder of wonders is now a balloon,
E'en the spectres are nothing tho' dancing in shrouds,
To the men who went up t'other day in the clouds.
     Sing ranta ra ra ra strange sight.

As they mounted above, Johnny Ball from below,
Cried Lord! who'd have thought it, to see where they go!
Look, look, don't they rise like a pair of sky rockets,
While the diver's keen eye kept a look on their pockets.
     Sing ranta ra ra etc.

Men women and children see, see, how they jam!
While the voyagers dine on the chickens and ham,
Who, tho' they could see all below like a push,
Epping Forest but look'd like a gooseberry bush.
     Sing ranta ra ra etc.

Sixty miles, like brave fellows, they trusted to fate,
And went all the time at a devil of a rate
When at length coming down near Colchester plains,
Hodge swore if they did that he'd blow out their brains
     Sing ranta ra ra, etc.

At last, after buffeting hills, roads and trees,
Terra firma receiv'd them, their journey to ease,
When the first house they called at to claim a protection
Says the master, Keep off, I'll not vote this election.
     Sing ranta ra ra etc.

Then, gossips, to gattle, nor keep your tongues mute,
Of the famous balloon, and likewise parachute,
And while the air subject, enlivens your gin
In gratitude drink to Monsieur Garnerin.
     Sing ranta ra ra etc.

Colchester
Printed by I Marsden, for S Carpue, London
*The word Amphitheatre has been misspelt by the printer.

The machinebreakers' riot at Little Clacton is the next of our locally produced ballads and appears to have been composed by a local poet, although the printer is unknown.

A FEW VERSES COMPOSED ON ACCOUNT OF
A RIOT
WHICH HAPPENED AT LITTLE CLACTON ON THE 8th OF
DECEMBER 1830
When three men were taken and transported for seven years and
three others sentenced to one years imprisonment –
my elopment to London and my being taken on New Years Day
– my Trial and my Imprisonment

It was on the eighth of last December
Which many of us well remember
When Little Clacton mob did rise
Which put the people in surprise
They rose up in the dead of night
Which put the people in a fright
For higher wages was their scheme
Likewise to break the lodge machine
Then in the morn we went straight way
And broke it up without delay
And thus we did begin our mob
But soon it proved a fatal job
For that same night mark what I say
They took three married men away
From wives and children and from home
And God knows wither they'll return
I being press'd to join the throng
For they took all both old and young
My adversary standing by
And mark'd what ere I did or say
A friend of mine to me did come
And said to me, "you'd better run
For there's a warrant out for you."
And what he said I found it was true
The night was cold the snow was sleating [?]   crease in paper
My wife and children all were weeping
When I from them was forc'd away
For there I dare no longer stay

I being put in such a fright
I left my home that very night
And at a friend's house near by
Three days and nights there did I lie
And when I heard they had searched for me
Thinks I now I must further flee
Then off to London I did go
My heart was filled with grief and woe
I did awhile in London dwell
And I hoped all things would end quite well
In hopes that I should get off clear
If I could get a half a year
And as I had got a situation
I very soon should left that station
But by some means it got about
And very soon they found me out
And on the morn of new years day
From London I was forc'd away
The Essex runner came so bold
And took me off to Springfield Gaol
Then soon for trial I did stand
The first thing was hold up your hand
Guilty or not the chairman cry'd
Guilty my lord I soon replied
Then they were all in consultation
And talking about transportation
My adversary look'd at me
No doubt but wished me across the sea
But so the chairman sentenced me
One year in Springfield Gaol to lie
Nine months to be kept to hard labour
The same he said to my neighbour
The last three months locked in my cell
In solitary lonely dwell
I hope the Lord will be my friend
And give me patience to the end
Now when in prison I did lie
And often wished for liberty
Our living work and bed was hard
And from all comforts were bar'd
We worked all weathers wet or dry
And were debar'd from liberty
Kept close all day until the bell

Did ring for us to take our cell
Then soon our keepers came around
To see if we were safe and sound
With keys in hand they walk so hard
And quickly were our door bar'd
All night the watchman goes his round
And lightly treads the hollow ground
The time of night to us he told
And gently cries out all is well
Then in the morn the bell does ring
And quickly up the turnkeys spring
Unbolt unlock and out we go
And for our bread stands in a row
Then to the treading mill we run
Until the clergyman does come
And then to chapel we prepare
To hear him read and say the prayers

Now to conclude and make an end
I don't wish any to offend
No doubt some folks will me blame
But 'tis the truth and can't be shamed
But as I have reached my home again
I hope I hope there to remain
Others may rise and they may scheme
I'll mob no more and break machines
But as the school boys copy says
Avoid alluring company

COMPOSED BY BENJAMIN GARDENER HACKSHALL
LITTLE CLACTON ESSEX

A large broadsheet was issued by T D Dutton of Chelmsford, whose printing works were in Conduit Street (*White's Directory of Essex 1848*) and later becoming J Dutton of Tindal Street, who was listed in trade directories from 1872 to 1931.

Titled *Hints for Farmers' Labourers*, the sheet's contents are a mixture of homely verses and a selection of 'do's and don'ts' for labourers to follow. Beneath the title and to either side of a woodcut of a farmyard are these verses:

The Peasantry of England

The Peasantry of England
Who till their native soil,
The loyal, true, and brave are they
Although they live to toil;
For they are England's own true men,
Her rural sons and free;
To drive the plough or wield the flail,
Or guard her liberty.

The Peasantry of England,
Whose wealth is their fire-side
Whose manly sons and daughters fair
Inspire their breasts with pride;
Whose only feast 'The Harvest Home',
Whose only pride 'The Fair',
Who love the hills and plains to roam
Free as the native air.

God bless the English peasantry!
Blest be their happy home;
God speed the plough, the loom, the sail,
A thousand years to come;
And may the manly pride they boast
Each gallant breast sustain
To guard from foes their native coast
And England's right maintain.

The sheet is signed and dated R.B. Writtle, January 20th, 1843. Compare the verses above with the reality of the conditions of the riots of the 1830s!

The Parliamentary Reform Bill was first introduced by Lord John Russell and Earl Grey in 1831, finally receiving Royal Assent on 7 June, 1832. Although it was a disappointment to the radicals, in that it still preserved the principle that it was property rather than persons which Parliament represented, there was some redistribution of seats. Many of the rotten boroughs (the number of inhabitants having shrunk until there was hardly anyone left to vote) lost their separate representation, while many of the big new industrial and commercial towns of the north (Manchester, Birmingham, Sheffield, Leeds, etc.) gained a representative.

While the Reform Bill was going before Parliament the London ballad printers were daily issuing new ballads on the subject, so it is hardly surprising that printers in the provinces issued their own, or reprinted popular ballads already in circulation.

The following was reprinted by S Shearcroft whose press was in High Street, Chelmsford (White's 1848).

A true picture of the times
or the
Poor man's consolations
From Reform!!

Come you that can tell us, we should just like to know,
What good our Reform Bill is likely to do,
After all their great promises the whole truth of the matter,
We can't find a poor man one farthing the better.

There was noble Earl Grey two years ago said,
That 'Reform would be sure to bring plenty of trade,'
Which would gladden the hearts of the labouring poor,
And yet – we are worse off now than before.

They pretended they'd dock the great placemen and pension,
But not a word about docking they mention,
If they take a tax off, the next thing that is done,
Is directly to clap a much bigger one on.

O Pitt! Billy Pitt! although you are dead,
Lord Althorne must certainly now wear your head!
Even Wellington himself durst never attempt,
On the whole house of commons to throw such contempt.

He pays no regard to the members' majority,
They are all forced to cringe to his Lordship's authority,
'Tis of no use their voting to take off a tax,
If they don't put it on again – woe to their backs!

If these are Reformers! Oh Russell! John Russell,
What good is your Reform Bill that has caused such a bustle,
Just point out the benefits that from it we've found,
Are the poor better off either in country or town?

See the starving mechanic begging hard for employment,
Though the wages he gets will afford no enjoyment,
For even those that have work are so rascally paid,
That they are in as much poverty as though they had play'd.

Look at the little shopkeepers in every street,
Who find it impossible to make both ends meet,
Eaten up by the taxes, devour'd by the rates,
The gaol or the workhouse is most likely their fate.

Oh blessed Reform, your benefits are great,
Especially if we could but get something to eat,
We might as well celebrate it with processions and dinners,
And starved ever since like poor hungry sinners.

Only look round the country, see the state of the poor,
See poverty stand at each cottager's door,
See the labouring toiling for ninepence a day,
Why don't you reform this! – Noble Earl Grey.

See the wretched poor pauper at work on the road,
Who would live by his labour if he possibly could,
Only view him at night in his comfortless home,
And ask his opinion of this blessed Reform.

See the ploughman as he whistles to drive away sorrow,
Or gnaw his brown crust on the ridge of a furrow,
Ask him if the Reform Bill has better'd his lot,
One meal in a week, and he'll say it has not.

And thus our reformed administration,
For these two years have contrived to humbug the nation,
And whilst we are most of us starving with hunger,
Lord Althorpe keeps telling us – to wait a bit longer.

Do something to be spoke of amongst you if you can,
You promised you would though you never said when,
Don't sit snaffling about nothing the whole sessions thro',
But honestly tell us what you mean for to do.

Do you call yourselves Whigs and friends of the poor?
Why even the Tories didn't humbug us more,
They brought poor John Bull to the brink of starvation,
And you try to keep him in the same situation.

Do away with your corn laws then trade will soon flourish,
Put a tax on machinery, men's labour to encourage,
Sweep off your great sinecures, your places, and pensions,
And then we'll believe you sincere in your intention.

Reprinted by J Shearcroft Chelmsford

The most prolific output of ballad sheets from local presses in Essex was at election times. A selection of these ballads and squibs has survived, if only to remind us that elections were at one time colourful affairs. With dinners for the gentry and beer for all and sundry, a good deal of bribery occurred as the prospective candidates vied with each other at the polls.

In the 1841 election Northern Essex was won by C G Round and Sir J T Tyrell and Southern Essex by T W Bramston and G Palmer, all Conservative candidates. This Parliament was called 'the Bribery Parliament' because of the extensive amount of corruption that took place at the poll.

In the days when we went canvassing
A Song
Sung on the Husting, by the Rejected of Bury and Essex

In the days when we went canvassing
A short time ago,
Of Whigs and Rads we did our best
To make a decent show
We laugh'd and talk'd, and laid our plans
(In privacy I mean),
And nought but sly and crafty coves
About us could be seen
       And thus we passed the pleasant time,
       Nor thought of care or woe,
       In the days when we went canvassing
       A short time ago.

All hearts were light, and eyes were bright,
The Tories all look'd gay,
Because at Bury we were lick'd
And forc'd to come away.
'Twas then we thought to try how much
The Essex Calves would hear,
We came and thought the prospect seemed,
Most flattering and fair.
      And thus we passed the pleasant time, etc.

We canvassed all the County round,
Amongst our friends most dear,
But then the secret all came out,
And hope was changed to fear.
We bawl'd 'The Queen' with all our might,
'Cheap Bread and Sugar' too,
But all this flummery and cant,
We found would never do.
      But still we passed the pleasant time, etc.

We saw that nought could us avail,
But gold from Cleveland's purse,
For arguments began to fail
And Voters turned perverse,
But when they sent the money down
With leave to spend the whole!
'Free of expense', our motto was,
And then we claim'd a poll.
      And so we passed the pleasant time, etc.

But should I ever pay again
A visit to this scene,
I'll call to mind, with blushing shame,
How great a tool I've been.
For only see how Essex men
Have laugh'd us all to scorn,
This day beyond a doubt has proved
Our hopes were all forlorn.
      And so, alas! the present time
      Is fraught with care and woe,
      Not as when we went canvassing
      A little while ago.
        Chelmsford July 10 1841
        Dutton, Printer, Chelmsford

A New Song to an Old Tune issued by J B Harvey of 166 High Street, Colchester, refers to the 1847 election. This ballad mentions a number of prominent political figures of the day. Joseph A Hardcastle (1815 – 99), formerly of Writtle, was M P for Colchester from 1847/52. Sir John T was Colonel John Tyssen Tyrell of Boreham House, who held one of the seats for the Conservatives in Northern Essex during the first half of the 19th century. Old Sir Henry refers to Sir George Henry Smyth of Berechurch Hall, who represented Colchester in 1826/30 and 1836/50. John Gurdon Rebow of Wivenhoe Park, Colchester, sat for Colchester for 1857/9 and then from 1865 until his death in 1870. The line in the first verse 'Have brought in a yellow and turned out a blue' alludes to the colours of the parties – yellow for the Whigs and blue for the Tories.

A
New Song to an Old Tune

Good news, said Jack Nokes to his neighbour Tom Stiles,
While quaffing their ale at a house in St Giles,
For we Colchester Burgesses, trusty and true,
Have brought in a Yellow, and turned out a Blue.
  For the Rights of our Town,
  Our Country and Crown,
  And the Rights of our Town.

We have struggled and fought, and conquered at length,
For Hardcastle's name is a tower of strength,
And while Old Sir Henry, Dissenters deride,
He shall never more sit with a Blue by his side.
  For the Rights of our Town, etc.

Good news, shouted Tom, for the County also,
And we'll now go to work for our neighbour Rebow,
We'll tell Sir John T that we'll give him the sack,
For we'll not have an Irishman, perch'd on his back.
  For the Rights of our Town, etc.

The name of a Soldier will never go down
With Essex Electors in County or Town.
No Strangers will suit us, but some one ye know,
And so we'll give Plumpers for Gordon Rebow.
          For the Rights of our Town, etc.

The Farmers confess that they can't understand
What the Major can do for their interests in Land,
They think he's more fit for a Riot to quell,
And they wish him safe home to his house at Pall Mall.
          For the Rights of our Town, etc.

Then hurrah for Rebow, he's the man we will choose,
Who will act independent in spite of his foes,
Our Land and our Commerce he will never betray,
But, for the good of us all, he will vote the right way.
          For the Rights of our Town, etc.

Harvey, printer, High Street, Colchester

Another of Harvey's ballads printed for the 1850 election signed John M----s (Lord John Manners, Colchester 1850/7) is a rather curious mixture of a letter to his public refuting an article printed in a newspaper and some lines from two poems; it just goes to show to what lengths elections were carried to in the war of words to win votes.

The Lover's Lament
To the Electors of Colchester

Gentlemen,
          You have no doubt seen my name in the Gazette, knowing the irreparable damage to my character that this m open, but to abandon the interesting connection between us, though in taking this desperate step I am
          Tortured by pangs which hopeless lovers feel
          As my anguish is too great to allow me further utterance, I beg to refer you to two of my English Ballads (pp 144 and 147) as a faithful expression of my sentiments.
          And remain,
                    Your Mournful, Disconsolate, Desolate and Undone
                    John M-----S

I ask thee not to think of me as now once more we part,
Another reigns supreme, I know on that dear throne thy heart,
The words of love I fain would breathe unspoken still remain,
I know thou lov'st another, and my humble love is vain.

____

Yet be it so! the time may come when he thou lovest now
Shall faithless prove and thou resent his false and broken vow,
When thou shalt sigh for love like mine, which time and chance defies,
Though buried deep in this love heart it now uncared for lies.

Then dearest, Farewell! At thy bidding I go
To brood in strange lands o'er my love and my woe,
But never believe, though for years I may range,
That my heart can grow cold, or my love it can change.

Harvey, Printer   166, High Street, Colchester

The last of this series of election ballads is an anonymously printed sheet, written for the 1852 General Election for an M P for Maldon, the results of which were:

Charles Du Cane	Con	370
Taverner John Miller		357
Thomas Barrett Lennard	Lib	351
Quintin Dick	Con	330

When the Parliamentary Commissioners made their enquiry they came to the conclusion that open and direct bribery took place to a greater extent than at any previous election, and that the poorer electors had been corrupted by wealthy men. Two candidates' expenses for drinks at Public Houses came to £5,000 and the cost of the beer drunk in Maldon and Heybridge amounted to £2,150. When Quintin Dick gave up in 1854 he had spent nearly £30,000 on electors at Maldon.*

*Essex in Parliament George Caunt 1969.

A case for 'Squinting Dick'
or
'The Miller and His Men'
air Who is that knocking at the door

The General Election is now drawing near,
And soon must the Members at the House appear,
Constituents be quick and get your work done,
I hear lots of Horses for the 'Derby' will run!
There'll be lots of knocking at the door!
John Bull will stand with a frown or a grin,
To keep intruders out or welcome friends in,
There'll be lots of knocking at the door, by the score!
There'll be lots of knocking at the door!

Men of Essex be sharp! Judge the false from the true,
And stick by those who will stick by you.
Let honourable Members your offices fill
Not the Dicky who's known by the length of his Bill,
There'll be lots of knocking at the door!
Knocking loud at the Parliament door!
Men of Maldon be firm! to your colours be true,
Like tars, jolly tars! be your motto 'True Blue'.
Tho' boasters may knock at your door and implore,
Let them go, as they came, from your door.

John Bull at the door will keep a look out,
Or, many will try to get past him, no doubt,
There's one hobbling up, but John has him pat,
'Before you go in' says he 'two words to that'
Who is that knocking at the door,
Who is that knocking at the door,
Is that you Sambo? 'No' it's Squinting Dick!
'Then you can't come in for you go so on tick!'
And it's no use knocking at my door any more,
It's no use knocking at the door!

Dick tries very hard to go in at the Door,
But Johnny won't flinch, as he's known him before,
'For you and your friend' says John 'are turn-coats,
Extremes must not meet, I'll have no split-votes!
Who is that knocking at the door?
Who is that knocking at the door?'

'Is that you, Sambo?' say Dick, 'No it's me.'
Says John Harriet Wilson, 'why you never paid she!'
        And it's no use knocking at the door any more!
        It's no use knocking at the door.

There next comes a man who again takes the field.
John Bull thinks he knows him, his face is concealed
He leans on Old Dick and tries to look big.
Says John 'Show your face, man, why you wear a Whig.'
        Who is that knocking at the door?
        Who is that knocking at the door?
'Is that you, Sambo?' 'I'm called a Lion' says he,
Says John 'It won't do, for you'll find Lennard's at Sea!
        And it's no use knocking at the door, any more!
        It's no use knocking at the door.

Now in come two men with a smart double knock,
John Bull sees at once that they're of a good stock,
'You're like Butlers' says he 'with good measures, not short
Come in thro' my portal for you can serve the Port!
        Who is that knocking at the door
        Who is that knocking at the door'
'Is that you, Sambo' 'No it's Miller and Du Caine.'
'Walk in' Says John 'you'll our rights maintain.'
        And you're both welcome in the door evermore
        You're both welcome in at my door.'

Another local ballad is a rather tongue-in-cheek comment on the inhabitants of Brentwood. The only requirement to have been included in this ballad was that your name began with 'B' and quite an amazing collection of trades and names has been made. I wonder if the author had a local *Kelly's Directory* at hand? Anyway, the sheet was printed by Meggy and Chalk of Chelmsford, who had been printing since 1796, when W Clachar took William Meggy and Thomas Chalk as partners; Clachar retired or died soon after, leaving the firm to Meggy and Chalk.

The B's of Brentwood
A Ballad

What a number of B's in Brentwood abound!
Not Bees who in waxen cells live,
But B's the initial of names in the town,
Who busy industriously strive.

Academus' grove is (opposed to all rules),
Transferred to the hill in the east,
Where a cluster of B's whose well-ordered schools,
Fix the generous thoughts in each breast!

First our old Grammar School wherein 'manners' are taught,
With 'learning and virtue' I trow,
There Despotic Bell reigns yet with kindness so fraught,
Who know him they love him I vow.

Round the corner Miss Bargeman her labour she plies,
Of girls she's a nice little pack.
Miss Brown further on the same calling supplies,
Right opposite lives Mr Black.

At your parties, so gay assistance you want,
Dan Bowerman ne'er will refuse,
Should your windows or doors require glazing or paint,
George Burtwell's the man you must choose.

Near to Burrell is Beazley with fish, – then there's Brown
In his snug little shop you'll espy,
At a window, that's loaded with fruit lower down
There lives Brewer, whose art is to dye.

See Barbrook, the elder, lean over his door,
He's a dealer in corn you must know,
In the next dashing window, his son from a store,
Makes of drapery goods quite a show.

But say who is this meekly bending with age?
My muse stop your hasty career.
If simplicity, industry, virtue engage,
To Baxter your homage pay here!

A Library's kept by S W Brown,
Where variety's brought you so pat,
Irish Porter he sells – Ale bottled in stone,
Walker's Sparkling Champagne – and all that.

Should you long for a steak to James Bell's you must rush,
For a dish here is Bailey at hand,
Or for pastry there's none can exceed Mrs Bush,
For drugs Belcher waits your command.

In number and weight all the Bacons I'll cram
In one verse or I ne'er shall get through,
For there's William and Joseph, and Isaac and Sam,
And the little Benjamin too.

In another trite verse I'll include with R Barnes,
(The shoemaker over the way),
Boreham, Buxton and Bateman, and Ballad, who earns
His bread by the binding of hay.

Binder, Byford and Bradley, are names I must add
To the list, though of no high renown,
And, oh strange, here's a Brand that belongs to the squad,
Which extinguished the lights of the town!

Mr Bush, at the Bull, he a song will prepare,
A son of Apollo is he,
He sure must be happy, when Bliss is so near,
Who loves both a catch and a glee.

Lowe-lane contains Batten, a tailor as staunch,
As e'er drew a stitch o'er a knee,
Sam Baker lives near him, who cut off the branch,
Which he sat on while lopping a tree. – (Fact.)

The stone-mason, Barnard, works down Warley Lane,
So do Bentley and Bolingbroke still,
And the bricklayer, Burgess, whenever in pain,
Seeks for cure in a Morrison's pill!

At the west of the town reside Butler and Bean,
And Branfoot, in physic they deal,
On their saddles they're bumping about, snow or rain,
Night or day, sickly pulses to feel.

But soft, there are others I cannot omit,
Briefly finished my jumble shall be,
These are Brindle and Britton, and Barker and Brett,
And there's Bright, - all beginning with B.

Now Braintree and Bocking, and Billericay,
Black Notley, Bradwell-near-the-seas,
Come show, if you can, if you can, then you may,
Such a conglomeration of B's.

Printed by Meggy and Chalk   Chelmsford

Local poet Harry Wheeler had at least one of his ballads printed for distribution. Harry worked for Canon Pertwee, the vicar of St James, Brightlingsea, and apparently could make up rhymes on the spur of the moment on any sort of subject. His broadside ballad called *A tale of an old, old well. Short account of the Well accident at Brightlingsea, May 1st 1899. How Wilson Webb was recovered after over eight hours entombment,* tells the story of Mr Samuel Wilson-Webb, who was an odd job builder in the town. He was in the process of looking at a well in East End Green on the outskirts of Brightlingsea, having been asked to deepen it and, so as to survey the lower parts, he had descended by ladder, when the walls collapsed. The two workmen with him went to get help and returned with a team of well-diggers from the local waterworks, who, after using an old 3-inch water pipe as an air-line, proceeded to dig another well alongside. Once down low enough, Mr Arthur Patrick, a small wiry man, burrowed through into the old shaft, giving the injured man brandy, probably for the pain. Webb was then winched out, to be treated by the local doctor, who had been standing by during the whole operation. As a result of his experience, Wilson-Webb lost all his hair, but continued to live in Colchester until he was 80.*

*From an article by Leslie Barnard in **Essex Countryside**, May, 1964. Ballad from A L Wakeling, Brightlingsea.

A Tale of an Old, Old Well
Short account of the Well Accident at Brightlingsea, May 1st 1899
How Wilson Webb was recovered after over eight hours' entombment.

There was once a well in Brightlingsea,
* But 'tis now closed up with soil,*
There's a startling tale concerning it
* That reaches many a mile,*
O read now the words I have written,
* For true is the tale they tell;*
You'll never again get Wilson Webb
* To deepen an old, old well.*

The whole of the town was excited,
 Early on the first of May,
When people heard the sad, sad news
 That a well had given way,
And deep down beneath the ruins
 With five tons over his head,
A Brightlingsea workman was buried,
 But, thank God! he was not dead.

It happened on a Monday morning,
 While shone the bright May sun,
And it caved in without warning,
 When his work he'd scarce begun.
He called to his fellow workmen,
 But his call was faint to them,
He told them to get help at once,
 And to work like Englishmen.

The terrified fellows then sped
 Off with all might and main,
And when they told their dreadful tale,
 Soon to thhe well help came.
Each helped to remove the debris,
 To get the poor man's head,
And soon a great crowd gathered,
 And each heart hung down like lead.

To ensure a constant air supply
  Was the foremost thing to do,
So they passed a three-inch water pipe
  Down to him, the debris through.
Straight down by the side of a ladder,
  The water pipe they led.
Thank God! for this very ladder
  Kept the great weight off his head.

And women stood there, watching,
  Trembling in every limb:
They could hear the poor man singing
  A verse of a well-known hymn,
His nerves were strong as ever,
  And his spirits never fell,
Whilst singing 'Rock of Ages,'
  At the bottom of that well.

Bricks, mortar, and other debris,
  Enclosed him all around,
He couldn't move a hand or foot,
  His head he could just turn round.
Reader, wasn't this enough
  To break a poor man's nerve?
'Twould turn the greatest villain's
  Thoughts to the God we serve.

He could hear the rescuers toiling,
  As he prayed to God on high,
O what would his wife and children do,
  He thought, if he were to die.
And all those who stood around there
  Thought he would see the light no more,
But the brave man trusted in Jesus,
  As he had always done before.

His wife and his bairns were waiting
  Some good or bad news to hear,
Those long eight hours and a quarter
  Seemed to the mother a year.
And he sent to her a message,
  By one who lived in the lane,
Telling her he trusted in Jesus,
  If he saw he ne'er again.

Then, after some hours of hard labour,
  They got to the poor man's head:
With brandy, in a feeding bottle,
  Fed him, as a babe is fed.
Soon then they got his shoulders
  Free from the bricks and stuff,
Then, passing a rope around him,
  They started pulling him up.

Inch by inch he began to rise,
  And cries of joy went forth –
Were heard (the cries of the people)
  In the East, West, South, and North.
And when they got him safely
  Above the up-turned ground,
With many excited 'Hurrahs!'
  The people gathered round.

Some did jump for gladness,
  Others did weep for joy.
'Thank God! Thank God! he's saved,'
  Was the almost frantic cry.
Then to the wife and children
  The good news almost flew,
As everyone in Brightlingsea
  Was glad when the truth they knew.

But he was a dreadful picture,
  That nobody can deny;
His clothes were torn and dirty,
  He'd a great gash over his eye,
And his face amd his round bald head
  Were white as a whitewashed wall,
He left one boot at the bottom,
  But that didn't matter at all.

Cheer after cheer did rend the air,
  Everyone did the same,
Men, women and children
  Cheered again and again.
Poor Webb had no more feeling
  In him than an old tin can,
But he still had that same brave heart,
  The heart of an Englishman.

They laid him upon a stretcher,
  He could neither move nor stand,
They picked him up and marched him off
  To a cottage near at hand,
The doctor there examined him,
  But he found no broken bones;
The people then departed,
  And walked them to their homes.

Poor Webb then home was taken,
  And quickly put to bed.
'He surely will recover,'
  The doctor safely said.
So the toil of the day was over
  Glad everyone did feel
And the rescuers turned them homeward
  To enjoy a hard-earned meal.

There was a well in Brightlingsea,
  That fell because 'twas rotten.
There's a startling tale concerning it
  That ne'er will be forgotten.
O read you the words I have written,
  For true is the tale they tell.
You'll never again get Wilson Webb
  To deepen an old, old well.
                                    HARRY WHEELER

Jabez Francis came to Rochford on 23 July, 1852, as foreman of a printing works owned by W H Jackson that had been moved from Romford to West Street, Rochford, in 1840. Eventually, Jabez bought the business, opening a branch shop in Southend in 1872 and making his son, William, the manager.

About this time he enlarged the West Street premises by taking over the adjoing shop to use as a stationers. he also started to make small iron presses with similarly made type, but was forced to stop when others copies his ideas in wood.

When the town pump was demolished in 1902, one of the Francis's composed and printed a ballad telling the story of the pump and naming the people who looked after it, like Asbey and Crowe, the plumbers who supervised the mechanism; Scott, the square's grocer who gave money for painting; and Rome and Bishop, ironmongers of the square, who maintained the ironwork.

The story of the pump began in 1820, when a public subscription was raised and a pump erected in the marketplace. The pump consisted of a cast iron casing, about a foot square and almost 8 feet high, with an enormous weight of about 20 lbs at the end of a long curved handle, and surrounded by ornamental posts and chains.

The well was dug by Good of Maldon, who bricked it to a depth of 80 feet. Sometime later the hole was bored a further 100 feet to increase the flow. At first the water was free; later it was put up for auction and a charge was made by the owners of $\frac{1}{4}$d. a pail and $\frac{1}{2}$d. a yoke (2 pails). When the pump was pulled down, the event was celebrated by a bonfire and tea and, of course, the ballad!

In Memoriam
Poor old Pump!

Since 1820 here I've stood,
And yielded of my best,
And now because I'm 'not so good',
Folks laugh at me and jest.

In good old Robert Asbey's time,
I well supplied your need,
And if I rusted in my prime,
He with good oil did feed,

And kept me in good order too,
As you must surely know,
But, if you doubt my word, then you
Had best consult Fred Crowe –

He knows, for many, many a time,
He's cleaned my inner man,
And painted me, nor did repine,
Deny it, if you can!

A quarter century ago
When I was feeling queer,
The late F Scott admired me so,
He nursed me for a year.

He had my works all scraped and cleaned,
And then cleared out my well,
So that the water brighter seemed –
But only for a spell.

For as Towns around me grew,
They tapped my vital spring,
And only those who know me, knew,
How hard I had to cling

To keep the very life in me
And yield the precious drink,
Alas! that I should live to see
My poor old body shrink?

My health it failed, and so they sent,
To Rome, but Bishop said –
'I am sure 'tis of no use Andrew –
'The poor old pump is dead.'

'The Water Mainds are laid you see,
'And soon from South Benfleet,
'The water will be coursing through
'The pipes in every street,'

'So let's erect a Fountain
'Upon the old Pump's site.
'Where naughty boys and wicked men
'May drink and ne'er get tight.'

And so, before they bury me,
They've adorned me with this wreath,
To those who have thus honoured me
I'll my last drops bequeath.

                              F.W.F.

The last of these local ballads was sent to me by Mrs Farrow of Loughton. This anonymous sheet has no imprint and was sold for 2d. Although not a true broadsheet of the accepted variety, it is still of some interest, if only to show how the 19th century ballad sheet was adapted for use, although not intentionally copies from its predecessor, but as a distant relative.

Mrs Farrow remembers Roper Witham pushing his fish cart and, he passed the Snakes Lane School (now Ray Lodge) railings, he called out 'Are we down-hearted?' and we children would shout 'No!'

The Gravedigger
Or   the Villager's Revenge

There was a man named Roper, a servant of the church,
They have been and given him the sack and left him in the lurch,
Not only did he srve it, but dug the graves as well,
And very often he got paid to toll the old church bell.
Now parishoners of Woodford Bridge it's a silly thing to do,
To let the Wardens sack this man who has been honest, brave, and true,

He Clipped the hedge, he cut the grass, these jobs he done so well,
And now you have given him the sack and sent his soul to ----
Years ago the Church caught fire, the flamses burst all around
Then shouts went up for Roper until he could be found
He came at last withh a bucket, to quench this awful blaze
It was through his mighty efforts the grand old church was saved.
You will sure to miss old Roper, when laying them to rest,
It's a shame to all the Village, as he tried to do his best,
He used some old knotted rope, instead of using webb
To release the knots, he on the coffin jumped, so the Claybury nurses said.

Now the Vicar and the Wardens not knowing what to do,
As discharging poor old Roper left them in a tidy stew
They put their heads together, you should hear the Vicar blare
I know a man who will do the job, I think his name is Hare.

How wise of you, the Wardens said, we will see him in the morn
He's just the man to cut the grass, he's been used to cutting corn.
Now 'Bunny' and his Lodger to the churchyard went so brave
With the tools upon their shoulders to dig the cowman's grave.
They dug it wide,they dug it deep, they dug it six foot long
With timber they got from mr Smith's to make it nice and strong.
The funeral over, the grave filled in, they made a decent job
Between him and the Lodger they will share out eighteen bob.
Now Roper said they could not do it, but they've done it all serene,
It's the biggest mistake ever Roper made, so he got no cause to scream,
Now Roper has got his living to get, so he is going to join his boys,
Selling fish around the streets, there will be an infernal noise.
He will shout fish alive and football dead as he pushes along his barrow,
His boys will sing that Hymn of Hate 'We shan't be around tomorrow.
Price Twopence

The most eccentric printer of broadside ballads in Essex was Charles Clark, born at Heybridge in 1806 and educated at Witham Place School.* Following his family tradition he became a farmer at Totham Hall, near Witham. He remained a bachelor all his life and occupied his spare time with his press, where he produced satirical songs and parodies that were privately circulated amongst his friends, neighbouring farmers and alehouse keepers.

He also reprinted old tracts and ballad sheets from his own library and was particularly interested in reprinting the works of Essex writers.

In 1833 Clark retired from farming and moved to Butterfly hall, Heybridge; by 1862 he had given up printing and writing to concentrate on collecting the books that eventually took over his house. He died on 17th March, 1880, aged 77, and was buried at Heybridge. Before his death he sold most of his library and, as he left no will, his affairs were reported to be under the administration of the Court of Chancery. As to his large collection of tracts and broadside ballads, it would be interesting to know what happened to them.

Charles Clark did not always sign his productions with his own name, but used pseudonyms, amongst his favourites being Mathus Merryfellow, Doggerel Drydog and Quinten Queerfellow. He would often, after signing his initials CC, put 'printed by the author at his private press'. But it was in his titles that he would excel in the use of words; for example, this heading of a 22-verse ballad:

Pithily preserved on paper for the pleasant Profit of all perverse wooers the perusal whereof will be right piteous.

Or again:

The Devising Doctors Documentary Delinquency.

His longest title consisted of one long alliterative sentence containing 75 words that began with the letter 'P': no word is used twice.

Another of his whims was the way he circulated his ballads. Any surplus he would tie to gas balloons

* **Essex Pride** Stan Jarvis, 1984

and, along with his address also in rhyme, he would release them and await a reply from whoever found them. Many of his ballads reflect his dislike of women and children, but his most remembered ballad is called *John Noakes and Mary Styles*, because it is in local dialect and one of the best examples of this type of writing.

For examples here, I have chosen two of his sheets that follow the more conventional broadside pattern.

Tiptree Races
(Established Upwards of 200 years ago)
To Tiptree we will go
By the author of the unlettered muse etc.

Come bustle! bustle! jump about
And let us moving be
Today for Tiptree we'll set out,
The races there to see
  Yes to Tiptree we will go, will go, will go
  To old Tiptree we will go.

From all the country round about
See! how they throng the way
But dolts, tis plain, at home remain
Upon St James' day
  All to Tiptree they will go, etc.

Some there will go to see the sport,
And on the horses bet
And some will go themselves to show
A beau or lass to get
  All to Tiptree they will go, etc.

But we will go old friends to greet,
As oft we've done before,
And the friendships form's in bye gone years
We'll there renew once more
  So to Tiptree we will go, etc.

'Success to Tiptre!' we again
Will drink with hearty cheer,
For our Races gay – like Christmas they
Come only once a year!
  Then to Tiptree we will go, will go, will go,
  To old Tiptree we will go.

July 1843.   *J.H.*

The prospectus for the Eastern Counties Railway was issued in 1834 with John Braithwaite as Engineer. The Parliamentary Bill received Royal Assent in 1836 to build a 5 foot gauge railway from East London to Colchester. The first section was completed in 1839 after much difficulty with marshes and expensive via- ducts in the London area. Trains ran from a temporary terminus in Mile End to another at Romford. The line was eventually completed and the first train ran to Colchester in 1843.

Eastern Counties Railway
The Line
A Parody
Air   The Sea
Not marble, nor the gilded monument
Of princes, shall out-line this powerful line.

Shakespeare

The line – the line – the Eastern Line!
The firm – the safe – the work so fine,
Without a jolt, without a bound
We're wafted through the scenes around,
With the wind we play – we mock each steed
While like the lightning's bolt we speed!

I'm on the line – I'm on the line
I am where comforts so combine
With the dome above, and the Lounge below,
And attendants whereso e'er we go:
If a storm comes o'er and rains earth steep,
No matter – I ride on and sleep!

I love – O! how I love to ride
By the power of Watts fierce, hissing tide!
Where each man's goal is reached so soon,
And whistles sound their warning tune,
To tell that cometh the station near
And why the course must now be clear.

I never pass the old highway o'er,
But I love the Railway more and more,
And back I fly to some timely train
Like our Braithwaite when his aid we'd gain,
And a glory to me it is indeed
For I so joy on the line to speed!

The hopes were few, and pockets closed,
At the time our line was first proposed.
thhe scheme was doubted, but men grew bold
When the Thorndon Lord so sought its gold!
And never were such ills to lurk
Asm at first, against great Braithwaite's work.

I have tried, sonce our first opening day,
Full many a buggy, coach, and 'shay',
With time to judge and power to range,
But never again shall sigh for change;
And now when I as a trav'ller shine
I go by our famous Eastern Line.

C.C.

Printed by Charles Clark(an amateur) at his private press

BIBLIOGRAPHY

Bratton, J S	The Victorian popular ballad
Brown, A F J	Essex at work
Burrows, J N	Essex units in the War, 1914-1919, vol.4
Chambers, R	Book of days
Dunn, G	The fellowship of song
Dyos, H J & Wolf, M	The Victorian city
Essex Libraries	Industries of the Eastern counties business review: Essex, 1888-90
Hindley, Charles	Curiosities of street literature
	A history of the Catnach Press
	The life and times of James Catnach
Holloway, J & Black, J	Later English broadside ballads, vol.2
Holsbaun, E J & Rude, G	Captain Swing
Horn, Pamela	Labouring life in Victorian countryside

Lloyd, A L   Folk song in England
Louis, James   Print and the people, 1819-1851
Mayhew, Henry   London labour and the London poor
Mingay, Gordon E   Rural life in Victorian England
Morsley, C   News from English countryside, 1750-1850
Newburg, V   Popular literature
Occomore, D M & Heath-Coleman, P
                           Transcripts of the Vaughan Williams Essex
                           folksong collection
Occomore, D M & Spratley, P
                           Bushes and briars
Pickering, M   Village song and culture
Shepherd, Leslie   The broadside ballad
                           The history of street literature
                           John Pitts, ballad printer of Seven Dials
Steer, F W   The history of the Dunmow Flitch
Thomson, R S   The development of the broadside ballad
                           trade & its influence upon the trans-
                           mission of English folksongs [PhD thesis,
                           Cambridge]
Vicinus, M   Broadsides of the industrial North
Williams, A   Folk songs of the Upper Thames

INDEX OF BALLADS

Source of ballads in the order they appear in the book. British
Library Catalogue references given where appropriate.

Five Complete Ken Crackers   Madden Collection of Broad-
                                    side Ballads, Cambridge

The New Warley Camp   Madden
Lancashire Militia Camp   Madden
Don't Touch my Girl   Compton   Collection   of
                                    Broadside Ballads,v.7,p.40
Fairlop Fair   Compton, v.2,p.167
Fairlop Fair   Sabine Baring Gould Col-
                                    lection of Ballads,v.1,p15
The Origins of Fairlop Fair   Baring Gould, v.1
Fairlop Oak   Essex Review. Oct.1936 v45
Song from the Blockmakers' Boat   Essex Record Office
The Spruce Mr Clark   Madden
Dunmow Flitch of Bacon   Steer: Dunmow Flitch
The Dunmow Flitch of Bacon   Hindley: Curiosities

Essex Dunmow and Bacon	Steer
Song of the Flitch	Steer
Epping Hunt	St Bride's Printing Library LS71
Chelmsford Agricultural Show	Madden
The Bonny Girl of Barking Town	Madden
Barking Town Quay	Valence House, Dagenham
Old Woman of Rumford	Baring Gould, v.8,p.52
Essex and Liberty	Madden
Trials & Execution of Rick Burners	St Bride's LS198
Dreadful Murder [Chigwell Row]	St Bride's SS288
Murder of Thomas Lowe	St Bride's SS362
The Wicked Woman of Chigwell	Hindley
Execution of John Moore	Bristol Ballads, v.2,p.431 Brit.Lib. 1800 c 20
A Warning to Young Persons	Bristol Ballads, v.2,p.421
Execution of Mary May	Mayhew: London labour
Copy of Verses on Drory and Jael Denny	Madden
Confession of Thos Drory	Madden
Trial and Confession of Thos Drory	St Bride's LS164
Lamentation of Thos Drory	Madden
Outrage & Murder on a Child at Purfleet	Thurrock Local History
Trial & Sentence of Death on Richard Coates	Museum
Lamentations of R Coates	Thurrock
Execution of Purfleet Murderer	Thurrock
Southend Crime [1] & [2]	Brit.Lib. 1875 d 9(25)
Dreadful Murder at Plaistow	Essex Record Office
We are Lucky Chaps at Waltham	Madden
Ilford Jail	Coakham: Across the years
King Coel	Essex Record Office
Garnerin's Balloon	Madden
A Riot at Little Clacton	Essex Libraries Ceefax
A True Picture of the Times	Madden
In the days we went a canvassing	Madden
A New Song to an Old Tune	Essex Record Office
The Lovers' Lament	Essex Record Office
A Cane for Squinting Dick	Essex Record Office
The B's of Brentwood	Essex Record Office
A Tale of an Old Well	Essex Countryside,May 1964
Poor Old Pump	Cryer: History of Rochford
The Grave Digger	Author's collection
Tiptree Races	Brit.Lib. T1529 (2)
Eastern Counties Railway	Brit.Lib. T1529 (2)